The
Phenomenon
of Anne Frank

JEWISH LITERATURE AND CULTURE

Alvin H. Rosenfeld, editor

The Phenomenon of Anne Frank

DAVID BARNOUW

Translated by
JEANNETTE K. RINGOLD

Indiana University Press

This book is a publication of

Indiana University Press
Office of Scholarly Publishing
Herman B Wells Library 350
1320 East 10th Street
Bloomington, Indiana 47405 USA

iupress.indiana.edu

Originally published as: David
Barnouw, *Het Fenomeen Anne Frank*
(Amsterdam, Bert Bakker 2012)
© 2012 by David Barnouw
English translation © 2018 by Indiana
University Press

Cover © KOBRA, photo by Elma
Verhey

Indiana University Press gratefully
acknowledges the support of the Dutch
Foundation for Literature

Nederlands
letterenfonds
dutch foundation
for literature

Cataloging information is available from
the Library of Congress.

ISBN 978-0-253-03220-1 (cloth)
ISBN 978-0-253-03219-5 (paperback)
ISBN 978-0-253-03218-8 (ebook)

1 2 3 4 5 23 22 21 20 19 18

Contents

Author's Note

IN ORDER TO MAKE THIS book more readable, no footnotes have been used, but where necessary, the text refers to the sources.

The two books that precede this one, *De Dagboeken van Anne Frank* (1986) [the Dutch critical edition of the diary] and *Anne Frank voor beginners and gevorderden* (1998) [Anne Frank for beginners and for advanced students] cite a lot of source material. The first book deals primarily with archival material, whereas the second book is based primarily on publications on the subject.

In addition to these two books with source material, there is an extensive collection of Anne Frank clippings consisting of seven archival boxes at the NIOD (Institute for War, Holocaust, and Genocide Studies), and an increasing amount of material is now becoming available on the internet.

Het Anne Frank Huis. Een biografie by Jos van der Lans and Herman Vuijsje, published in 2010, also contains a wealth of material.

Chapter 1 is based partly on Barnouw/Van der Stroom/Paape, *De Dagboeken van Anne Frank* (Amsterdam, 1986) and Barnouw/Van der Stroom, *Wie verraadde Anne Frank?* Den Haag, 2003).

Chapter 2 is based partly on Barnouw/Van der Stroom/Paape, *De Dagboeken van Anne Frank* (Amsterdam, 1986) and Schroth, *Das Tagebuch* etc. (2006).

Chapter 3 is based partly on Barnouw/Van der Stroom/Paape, *De Dagboeken van Anne Frank* (Amsterdam, 1986), Graver, *An Obsession with* etc. (1995), and Melnick, *The Stolen Legacy* etc. (1995).

Chapter 4 is based partly on Barnouw, *Een delicaat onderwerp* etc. (1995).

Chapter 5 is based partly on *De Dagboeken van Anne Frank* (1986) and later newspaper clippings.

Chapter 6 is based partly on Barnouw, *Anne Frank voor beginners and gevorderden* (1998).

Chapter 7 is based partly on a symposium that was organized in 2007 by the NIOD and the Anne Frank House on the occasion of the seventieth anniversary of *Het Achterhuis*.

Translator's Note

I HAVE FOLLOWED THE AUTHOR's lead. When the author says that he has not used footnotes and has based various chapters partly on previous publications, I have done the same. The principal source for much of this book was the critical edition of the diary. Instead of the Dutch critical edition, *De Dagboeken van Anne Frank*, I have used the English version published in 2003, *The Diary of Anne Frank: The Revised Critical Edition*.

De Dagboeken van Anne Frank—to avoid confusion with various translations, I have not translated this title when it refers to the Dutch publication. When the "critical edition of the diary" is used, it refers to either the Dutch or the English version.

Het Achterhuis—the title of the original 1947 publication of Anne's diary. To avoid confusion with various translations, I have not translated this title when it refers to the Dutch publication.

When quoting from Anne Frank's diary, I have used *The Diary of a Young Girl: The Definitive Edition*. New York: Doubleday, 1995, which was edited by Otto Frank and Miriam Pressler and translated by Susan Massotty.

The Anne Frank Stichting in Amsterdam, a foundation that was established in 1957 and manages the museum at 263 Prinsengracht is called the Anne Frank House.

The Anne Frank Fonds in Basel is called the Anne Frank Foundation, or the Foundation.

NIOD is the Netherlands Institute for War, Holocaust, and Genocide Studies (formerly RIOD—Netherlands State Institute for War Documentation).

Introduction

ON SUNDAY, APRIL 27, 2014, amid great public interest, a cutting from the famous "Anne Frank tree" was planted in the garden of the Capitol in Washington, DC. Many seedlings of this chestnut tree had been cultivated after it blew down in the summer of 2010. The United States received eleven in addition to the one next to the Capitol. Cuttings were planted on the Boston Common, in Liberty Park in New York City, and in the Clinton Presidential Center in Little Rock to mention a few. The main theme at these 'tree-plantings' was Anne's indomitable spirit enduring through her book and plantings although her life was cut tragically short.

A week later, on May 8, 2014, I was present at the world premiere of the new play, *ANNE*, in a theater especially built for it in Amsterdam. The Dutch king, the minister of education, the mayor of Amsterdam, and other dignitaries were all present. It was a significant evening that had been anticipated for a long time, but it was also surrounded by discussions about whether going to see *Anne* could be considered a "nice evening out." The most important discussions revolved around the question to whom Anne actually belonged and who should speak for her.

This was clear until the death of Anne's father, Otto Frank, in 1980; on being asked, he explained what Anne had meant. Subsequently, it was the Anne Frank House in Amsterdam, the administrator of the Annex on Prinsengracht, which guarded her legacy.

With a new play, an organization that had remained in the shadows came forward, claiming to administer Anne Frank's legacy. This organization is the Anne Frank Foundation in Basel, which was established by Otto Frank in 1963. The Foundation administered the money from the royalties of the diary and passed it on to good causes. How much money has come in and has been given away during the more than fifty years of the existence of the Foundation is unknown.

Several times during the past decades, the Anne Frank Foundation backed a film production about Anne Frank while the Anne Frank House was against it, or vice versa. The Foundation occasionally instituted legal proceedings against the Anne Frank House when tensions between the two organizations mounted. The Anne Frank Foundation gave very little money for the extensive renovation of the Annex on Prinsengracht made at the end of the twentieth century. The outside world noticed little of the internal bickering, and it seemed as though the Anne Frank Foundation and the Anne Frank House were jointly protecting Anne's legacy against wrongdoers.

In 2007, the chairman of the Foundation, Anne's first cousin, the recently deceased Buddy Elias, handed a large number of historic letters, documents, and photos to the Anne Frank House. This "Frank family collection" was meant as a loan, and Elias thought that the Anne Frank House would take good care of these materials. It seemed the high point of close cooperation between the Anne Frank House and the Anne Frank Foundation, but four years later that cooperation seemed over. The Foundation had requested the return of the loaned materials, but the Anne Frank House did not comply. The Foundation went to court and was proved right. When you borrow something, you have to honor a request to return it. It turned out that there were extensive plans by the Anne Frank Foundation to add a *Familie Frank Zentrum* to the Jüdische Museum in Frankfurt. They now feel that Frankfurt is more important for Anne Frank than Amsterdam because she was born in that German city. Yves Kugelman, an active member of the Foundation Board, emphasized the extent to which Anne Frank's legacy is being squandered at Prinsengracht in Amsterdam.

In addition to the new museum extension, the Anne Frank Foundation was also responsible for the docudrama *Meine Tochter Anne Frank*, which was broadcast in February 2015 on the first public channel of German television. The second public channel, which also wanted to make an Anne Frank movie, was put under pressure by the Foundation and stopped the production. In 2016 a German language movie about Anne Frank appeared in the theaters; it was produced by the German Zeitsprung Pictures in cooperation with the Foundation. At the outdoor shooting scenes in Amsterdam, there were warning signs: "Attention! Production is related to WWII and can be experienced as distressing." In addition, the Anne Frank Foundation has asked Israeli movie director Ari Folman (*Waltz with Bashir*, 2008) to make an animated feature film about the life of Anne Frank.

All these things were set up by the Foundation, without involving the Anne Frank House, and the same goes for the *Anne Frank Gesamtausgabe* (more than 800 pages) published in 2014 and a scholarly Anne Frank Project at the University of Göttingen.

IN AMSTERDAM THE ANNE FRANK House and the Huygens Institute are collaborating on the scholarly editing of new historical research into Anne Frank's manuscripts. Originally, the Anne Frank Foundation also participated, but it has pulled out. The NIOD, which published the first critical edition of Anne Frank's writings (Doubleday, 1986), was left out of this for a long time. That was odd because the Huygens Institute, just like the NIOD, is part of the Royal Netherlands Academy of Arts and Sciences.

On March 12, 2015, an *in memoriam* for Edith, Margot, and Anne Frank appeared in English in a Dutch newspaper; it was signed by the Anne Frank Foundation and the family.

All these activities indicate a great dynamism on the part of the Foundation in Basel, which realizes that copyrights don't last forever. In 2015 it was seventy years since Anne died in Bergen-Belsen, and the copyright on *Het Achterhuis* expired at the end of that year. It's more complicated in the case of her original texts because all her diary texts were published for the first time in 1986. Early in 2016, a discussion flared up between lawyers and copyright scholars because a lot of money is involved. The Foundation showed immediately that they are the sole legitimate heirs of Anne Frank.

At this point the Anne Frank House also announced some news. In March 2015 it published a research report stating that the Frank girls didn't die in Bergen-Belsen at the end of March 1945: "Their date of death should be . . . earlier, sometime in February. Exactly when, we don't know." Of course that was old news, for the critical NIOD edition of 1986 had already mentioned that there were indications that they died at the end of February or early in March.

The old question, "What kind of girl was Anne Frank?" has been replaced by the new question, "To whom does Anne Frank belong?" The question of how her diary became famous worldwide remains unanswered.

Thirty years earlier, in 1979, when I started work at the NIOD, I had of course heard of Anne Frank, but I'd never read her diary *Het Achterhuis*. I read a lot about the Second World War, and my parents told me plenty, but a book written by a girl still remained a girls' book for me.

Anne's father, Otto Frank, died in August 1980 in Switzerland—in Birsfelden near Basel. His death was recorded, and the newspaper clippings about it were put in a clipping file (KB 1 7893) that the NIOD kept about him and many others. A short time later, the Institute received a letter from a lawyer in Basel, stating that according to Otto Frank's will, the NIOD had inherited all of Anne Frank's manuscripts and three photo albums. In addition, all the objects that Otto Frank had loaned to the Anne Frank House during the past decades had been transferred to NIOD ownership as well.

The hopeful thought that the NIOD would also acquire the copyright income was soon proved wrong; for many years, it had been collected by the Foundation in Basel. That remained the same, even after Otto's death.

NIOD decided, after an internal consideration and deliberation with the Ministry of Education, Culture and Science, to publish the different versions of Anne's diary in their entirety with introductory chapters. I joined the small team in charge of this project, which included the then director, Harry Paape, and my colleague Gerrold van der Stroom.

This decision had a great influence on the rest of my working life. I collaborated on the scholarly publication *De Dagboeken van Anne Frank*, the Dutch critical edition of the diary that would later appear in other languages. And I was becoming an expert in an international phenomenon with worldwide interest. Until then, the Anne Frank House, established in 1957, which managed the museum on Prinsengracht, had taken care of Anne's spiritual legacy. Now, in addition to the Anne Frank House, the NIOD became a part of the team. Because the NIOD was now the owner of the diaries, it had become responsible for them and regularly had to check on them and the loose diary sheets that lay in the display cases of the exhibition hall of the Anne Frank House. The fact that, for years—armed with display case keys—I had come every trimester to turn the pages of the diary to prevent discoloration, showed that the Anne Frank House had to share the responsibility for Anne's legacy.

Because of its public function and the impact that the Second World War continues to have, the staff members of the NIOD are asked about many subjects in addition to Anne Frank. Simply answering questions didn't satisfy me; therefore I started to write about various aspects surrounding her. It struck me that there was little analytical or critical writing about the phenomenon of Anne Frank. Far and away most of the publications were articles and books in which the diary was used for educational purposes. Almost no one asked how a completely unknown girl, killed in Bergen-Belsen, had become an icon within a few decades.

Meanwhile the diary has been translated into more than sixty languages, more than twenty million copies have been sold, and the Annex, Anne's place of hiding, now attracts more than a million visitors each year. In addition, hundreds of thousands of people in numerous countries have seen an Anne Frank exhibition. This massive interest and the corresponding manifestations caused me to use the term "Anne Frank industry"—not in a negative sense, but analogous to the earlier term "Holocaust industry." I had become part of it myself. The term "Anne Frank industry" led to conflicts with the leadership of the Anne Frank House, which disapproved of many of my statements and publications about Anne Frank. The director of the Anne Frank House tried unsuccessfully several times to have my director(s) silence me. It is also because of such conflicts that I have exercised restraint in describing matters in which I was directly involved.

Lecture tours in the United States, where I talked to college and high school students about Anne Frank, taught me more about the international character of the phenomenon of Anne Frank. In 1998, I published *Anne Frank voor beginners en gevorderden* (Anne Frank for beginners and for advanced students), a more or less chronological overview of half a century of Anne Frank in the Netherlands and the world. Since then a number of interesting studies about Anne Frank have been written and more historical research has been done in various archives, including those of the Anne Frank House and the Foundation. Because of this, several new theories have been put forth about the betrayal. And, also in 1998, unknown diary sheets surfaced in which Anne criticizes her parents' marriage.

In 2004 Anne's name was entered in a Dutch TV show to compete for the title of "greatest Dutch citizen of all time," but it was discovered that she had never had Dutch citizenship. She was born a German, but the Nuremberg race laws of 1935 had made her and all other German Jews stateless. Dutch members of parliament scrambled to give Anne Frank the Dutch nationality posthumously. Three years later, the same thing happened in the United States, where a discovery of letters led to proposals to give Anne Frank American citizenship posthumously.

Only ten years after her death, in the 1950s, "diary-Anne" became a "stage-Anne," an almost American teenager who believed in the goodness of people. Since the end of the twentieth century, Anne has become more Dutch than ever. Her authorship has become more central, and from the somewhat disparaging designation as girls' literature, *Het Achterhuis* now approaches the canon of real literature.

The fall of "her" chestnut tree in August 2010 led to an international media hype. Such things take our attention away from what is most important: Anne Frank's persecution and ultimate death because she and her family were Jewish. How and why did an unknown girl from Amsterdam develop posthumously into an international icon in a relatively short time? In *The Phenomenon of Anne Frank*, I try to answer that question. I discuss numerous matters around Anne Frank and her connection to them, the publication of *Het Achterhuis* and the translations, the play and the movie, the attacks on authenticity, the many claims on Anne, her authorship, and the continuation of her legacy in the twenty-first century.

—David Barnouw, Amsterdam

The
Phenomenon
of Anne Frank

Frankfurt—Amsterdam—Bergen-Belsen

Dearest Kitty[,]

So there we were. Father, Mother and I, walking in the pouring rain, each of us with a schoolbag and a shopping bag filled to the brim with the most varied assortment of items.

EVERYONE KNOWS WHO WROTE THIS: Anne Frank, the world-famous diary writer. In 1942 she left her house on Merwedeplein in Amsterdam with her parents. Her older sister, Margot, had already gone ahead to the office and warehouse of Otto Frank at 263 Prinsengracht. Since 2005, Anne stands on Merwedeplein, cast in bronze, carrying two bags, and looking back at the house that she would never see again.

Frankfurt am Main

The Frank family officially moved to Amsterdam in August 1933, but for Otto, Anne's father, it wasn't the first time he lived there. Otto Heinrich Frank, born on May 12, 1889, in Frankfurt am Main, was the second son of bank director Michael Frank (1851–1909) and Alice Betty Stern (1865–1953). The family, with three sons and two daughters, was liberal Jewish and not religiously observant. Upon Michael's death, his widow, Alice Frank, took over the business. Their son Otto was in the United States at the time, visiting Nathan Strauss Jr. (1889–1961), a college friend from Heidelberg who lived in New York. Nathan Sr. and his brother Isidor were coowners of Macy's. Strauss came from a family of Jewish emigrants from Germany, and Otto visited him several times.

During the First World War, Otto joined the German army and became lieutenant of an artillery regiment that was deployed at the western front where he eventually received the Iron Cross. Both of Otto's brothers also survived the war at the front, but unlike them, Otto didn't return home until several months after the German surrender. Supposedly, Otto returned two horses that his unit had seized from a Belgian farmer because he had given his "word of honor as a German officer" to do so. Another version of the story claims that he returned the horses to Pomerania, in the eastern part of Germany, but this detour of hundreds of kilometers seems too far-fetched to be true.

The German defeat and the subsequent economic inflation had an adverse effect on the family's bank. In the expectation that Amsterdam might be a good place for business, the family sent Otto to Amsterdam so that he would become involved in foreign currency trading and the banking business. During those years, Amsterdam was Germany's gateway to the international capital market. At the end of 1923, the M. Frank & Zonen Bank was officially established, and Otto went to live at 604 Keizersgracht, where the bank was located as well. Johannes Kleiman (1893–1959), who was nine years older than Otto and would later play an important role in his life, was one of the bank's authorized agents. The bank was not successful; the end was near after only a year, although it would take another five years before it was actually liquidated. Otto had lived in Amsterdam for only a short time before returning to the family home in Germany.

In the spring of 1936, at the age of thirty-six, Otto married twenty-five-year-old Edith Holländer (1900–1945). Edith was the daughter of Abraham Holländer (1860–1928), a well-to-do Jewish manufacturer, and Rosa Holländer-Stern (1866–1942). The Holländer family, who lived in Aachen, was more religious than the Frank family and kept kosher, but Edith had attended a Christian girls' high school. The wedding ceremony took place in the synagogue in Aachen and was followed by a celebration in a well-known Aachen hotel. On their honeymoon, they went to San Remo, Italy, where they had met.

After their honeymoon, Otto and Edith first lived in the Frank family home in Frankfurt, where their oldest child, Margot Betti, was born on February 16, 1926. A year later, the family moved to another house in Frankfurt so they could raise their daughter in a more liberal and modern way, without interference from the family. On June 12, 1929, Annelies Marie, called Anne, was born. At the time, Otto was again working for the family bank, but the business had not improved. His brother-in-law, Eric (1890–1984), who also worked at the bank, moved to Switzerland in the fall of 1929 to set up a Swiss branch of the Opekta-Werke. This was a subsidiary of the Pomosin-Werke in Frankfurt, which manufactured and distributed pectin. This gelling agent was a kind of resin that was used primarily as a binding agent in the production of jam and was therefore quite seasonal, and pectin was especially in demand after the fruit harvest. Eric established himself in Basel and was followed by his wife and children. In addition to the branch in Frankfurt, there was now a Frank branch in northern Switzerland.

Otto Frank's young family was affected not only by the economic consequences of the world crisis of 1929, but also by the rise of Hitler's National Socialist German Workers Party (NSDAP). Because of strict foreign currency regulations, the bank, which traded in international securities, got into greater financial difficulties, and at the end of January 1923, all activities of the Frank family bank were stopped. In 1933 the Nazis had achieved a great victory in the municipal elections of liberal Frankfurt, and the Jewish mayor was forced to resign. Jewish municipal employees were dismissed, and before long, Jewish children were separated from non-Jewish children in schoolrooms. Life became increasingly difficult, and there seemed to be no end in sight.

Like many other Jews, Otto Frank wanted to leave Germany, perhaps temporarily—until Germany had once again become a democratic country. Time was pressing, and the Netherlands were a logical choice as a democratic neighbor that had no open—let alone state-sponsored—anti-Semitism. Moreover, the country had remained neutral during the First World War. In addition, Otto knew Amsterdam somewhat because of his earlier stay. With the support of his brother-in-law, Otto was able to establish a branch of Opekta in the Netherlands.

Amsterdam

Otto had two main objectives in Amsterdam: to set up and establish his business and to find a place for his family to live. At first, he was alone in the city because his wife and two daughters were staying with his mother-in-law in Aachen (his father-in-law had died in 1929). The Dutch Opekta Company was located at 120 Nieuwezijds Voorburgwal in the center of the city. There were start-up problems because in Utrecht, not far from Amsterdam, a competing Pomosin company existed. But Otto decided to specialize in the sale of small quantities of pectin to housewives for jam-making. In addition to these direct sales, the product was to be sold in pharmacies, both in bottled liquid form and small bags of powder. Some Opekta advertising material has been saved, and it shows that the 1938 Opekta movie that was used as a training film for housewives was quite modern. It demonstrated how one should carefully handle the exact quantities of fruit, sugar, and pectin to have a good result. Miep Gies (1909–2010), one of Otto's staff members, played a role in this movie.

Miep was born in Vienna as Hermine Santrouschitz, and after the First World War she was sent to the Netherlands with a group of undernourished Austrian children to recuperate. Of course, they were supposed to return to Austria afterward, but Miep remained with her host family, the Nieuwenburgs, first in the university city of Leiden and later in Amsterdam.

Within a year, Opekta's business premises were too small, and the company moved to 400 Singel, where it stayed for six years. At the end of 1940, there was a third move, this time to 263 Prinsengracht. During the war, the building on Singel would become the headquarters of one of the Amsterdam Defense Section (WA) regiments, the armed hooligans of the Dutch Nazi party (NSB).

Meanwhile, Otto Frank sublet the third floor of 24 Stadionkade, but because it was too small for the whole family, he continued to look for an apartment. He found one that was again on the third floor, this time at 37 Merwedeplein, a quiet square in a new neighborhood of Amsterdam-Zuid, which was dominated by the *Wolkenkrabber* (skyscraper), the tallest residential building in the Netherlands at the time. This new housing development attracted political and Jewish refugees from Germany—if they had enough money to live there.

The family was reunited early in 1934, and this was the start of a relatively happy period for them. Edith, in particular, had a difficult time, however; she was homesick for Germany and missed her family and friends. She maintained close contact with her mother in Aachen, who came to live with the family in March 1939. It was rather exceptional that Edith's mother, Rosa, had received a residence permit, since the Netherlands had tried for some time to keep its borders closed to refugees. In the summer of 1941, Edith's mother became ill and died of cancer that same year. Julius (1894–1967) and Walter (1867–1968), Edith's two brothers, had left for the United States in 1938.

Otto and Edith had many German friends, refugees like them, but through his work, Otto also had many non-Jewish friends and acquaintances. Edith became active in the emerging liberal Jewish community, and—unlike her husband—she regularly went to the synagogue. Margot and Anne, eight and four years old respectively, obviously integrated more easily than their parents when they arrived in Amsterdam. They didn't attend a Jewish or an ordinary public school; instead, their parents chose the progressive Montessori education. The girls had friends, played in the street, went to the beach, and even went abroad on vacation. The Netherlands had become their second country, and they surely didn't worry much about the German *Reichsbürgergesetz* (citizenship law in Nazi Germany) of September 1935. That law stated, among other things, that German Jews no longer had citizenship. For Otto and Edith, it was the latest evidence that anti-Semitism in Germany was becoming increasingly vicious and that they had done the right thing by leaving for the Netherlands. Otto Frank seemed to be quite at home, witnessing his short biography with a photo in *Persoonlijkheden in het Koninkrijk der Nederlanden in Woord en Beeld* (Notable personalities in the kingdom of the Netherlands in words and pictures) published in 1938—a hefty and uncritical volume of more than 1,700 pages, in which one could be included at a charge. But should they perhaps move on—to Great Britain or the United States? In 1938 Otto filled out their first application for emigration to the United States, the first of many desperate attempts to keep ahead of Hitler.

Because Opekta was still no gold mine, Otto set up the Pectacon Trading Company, which would be involved with herb mixtures for sausages. Johannes Kleiman did the bookkeeping, and Victor Kugler (1900–1981), one of the first employees, became an authorized agent. Miep Gies, who had started as a temp worker, soon developed into an all-around employee and was assisted by Bep Voskuijl (1919–1983). Hermann van Pels (1898–1944), who had fled Osnabrück, became the most important person in Pectacon. In Germany he had been in charge of a similar company with his father, but increasingly menaced by the anti-Jewish measures, Hermann had left for the Netherlands in 1937 with his wife, Auguste (1900–1945), and their son, Peter (1926–1945). Otto had already made plans to establish a new company overseas, but as he wrote to his friend Strauss in the United States at the end of April 1941: "All these plans had to be given up by the war, and I had to stay where I was."

The war, which broke out in September 1939, did not yet have direct consequences for the Netherlands, and most inhabitants hoped that the country would remain neutral as it had during the First World War. But the threat increased, and the Frank girls were also aware of it. Through their school they had American pen pals, Juanita and Betty Wagner from Danville, near Burlington, Iowa. On April 27, 1949, fourteen-year-old Margot wrote in a letter: "We often listen to the radio, for these are exciting times and it doesn't feel safe as a small country to share a border with Germany."

On May 10, 1940, the war came to the Netherlands after all, and most of the armed forces capitulated after five days. Since the Germans considered the Dutch a "Germanic Brudervolk," it seemed at first that the Germans meant well with the Dutch, and even the overwhelming majority of the Jews breathed a sigh of relief. But not for long.

A Diary

For her thirteenth birthday, Anne received an autograph album that she started to use as a diary. Her first musings were dated June 12, 1942: "I hope I will be able to confide everything to you, as I have never been able to confide in anyone, and I hope you will be a great source of comfort and support." In her diary, Anne described herself as a sociable chatterbox who made things difficult for her teachers, who had lots of girlfriends and also "many admirers." Anne started at the Montessori nursery school and attended this school until the summer of 1941 when she—like her sister and all other Jewish students in the Netherlands—was forced to transfer to a Jewish school, in her case, the Jewish Lyceum.

On June 20, 1942, Anne wrote a short summary of the previous four years:

Our lives were not without anxiety, since our relatives in Germany were suffering under Hitler's anti-Jewish laws. After the pogroms in 1938 my two uncles (my mother's brothers) fled Germany, finding safe refuge in North America. My elderly grandmother came to live with us. She was seventy-three years old at the time.

After May 1940 the good times were few and far between: first there was the war, then the capitulation and then the arrival of the Germans, which is when the trouble started for the Jews. Our freedom was severely restricted by a series of anti-Jewish decrees: Jews were required to wear a yellow star; Jews were required to turn in their bicycles; Jews were forbidden to use streetcars; Jews were forbidden to ride in cars, even their own; Jews were required to do their shopping between 3 and 5 P.M.; Jews were required to frequent only Jewish-owned barbershops and beauty parlors; Jews were forbidden to be out on the streets between 8 P.M. and 6 A.M.; Jews were forbidden to attend theaters, movies or any other forms of entertainment; Jews were forbidden to use swimming pools, tennis courts, hockey fields or any other athletic fields; Jews were forbidden to go rowing; Jews were forbidden to take part in any athletic activity in public; Jews were forbidden to sit in their gardens or those of their friends after 8 P.M.; Jews were forbidden to visit Christians in their homes; Jews were required to attend Jewish schools, etc. You couldn't do this and you couldn't do that, but life went on.

From December 1, 1940, onward, both Pectacon and Opekta had been located at 263 Prinsengracht, and Otto Frank did his best to prevent or at least delay the "aryanization" of his company by the Germans. Aryanization meant that the occupier would expropriate the Jewish owner and appoint an acting manager who would be in charge. Otto arranged for Pectacon to be transferred to Kleiman's name so that the company was no longer in Jewish hands. However, the Germans realized that this was only a sham; the transfer was canceled, and Pectacon was liquidated. A lawyer from Amsterdam, A. R. W. M. Dunselman, helped them with this, just as Miep and her husband, Jan Gies (1905–1993), also helped them.

In addition, Otto made attempts at emigration, and he involved his old friend Nathan Strauss in his attempt to come to the United States, if necessary, by way of Cuba. In the April 1940 letter mentioned earlier, Otto says: "No one knows if there is still a chance to leave Europe when you receive this letter." In a letter from September 1941, he writes, "Edith urges me to leave by myself or with the children," and he repeats these words a month later. When the United States became involved in the war in December 1941, that way was obviously blocked. On January 20, 1942, Otto made another attempt at emigration, this time through the Jewish Council of Amsterdam and the *Zentralstelle für jüdische Auswanderung* (Central Agency for Jewish Emigration). The main purpose of this agency was to give Jews false hope for emigration, because at that point it was out of the question for all but a few exceptions. At the same time, Otto was busy furnishing a hiding place for himself and his family in the annex of his office and warehouse on Prinsengracht. With the help of friends, he had transported furniture, bedding, clothes, food, and whatever might be necessary for survival.

In Hiding

By this time, almost all Jews in the Netherlands were registered, systematically reduced to poverty, often out of work, and isolated from their non-Jewish surroundings. In addition, since May 1942, they had to wear a yellow star. In the eastern part of the Netherlands, near the village of Westerbork, a reception camp of the same name was set up for Jewish refugees from Germany. Originally, this camp was to be built in the center of the Netherlands, but Queen Wilhelmina objected because it would be close to her palace. The local tourist office was also against it because it would scare away tourists. In the second half of 1942, this remote reception camp became a "transit camp" for Jews and would be their last residence on Dutch soil. The Germans had taken all necessary measures for the first deportations "to the East" to start; of course, it was not mentioned that the deportees' final destinations would be the Auschwitz or Sobibor extermination camps. The first group to be called up consisted primarily of German Jews who were to report for "work in the East." Among them were young people between fifteen and eighteen years old, and on July 5, 1942, sixteen-year-old Margot received a call-up to report. For the Frank family, this was the immediate cause for going into hiding in the so-called Annex at 263 Prinsengracht together with the Van Pels family. Almost half a year later, the Jewish dentist Friedrich Pfeffer (1889–1944), who had fled Berlin in 1938, would join them.

These eight persecuted Jews were able to stay in hiding until August 4, 1944, with the help of Johannes Kleiman, Victor Kugler, Miep Gies, and Bep Voskuijl. Others were involved too, such as Jan Gies, and helpful suppliers in the neighborhood. This situation was exceptional because it was seldom that an entire Jewish family went into hiding together. Most often, Jews took refuge in other people's homes where there was space for only one or two people to hide and parents often let their young children go into hiding while they themselves did not.

Anne had taken her diary along; it was the first thing she packed when they went into hiding. Through her diary we now know what the life of those hidden Jews looked like and how Anne went through accelerated puberty. She wrote down all the ups and downs, her bickering with her mother, and her great affection for her father. "I'm crazy about him. I model myself after Father, and there's no one in the world I love more" (November 7, 1942). Although she initially thought that Peter, the son of the Van Pels couple, was a dull boy, later she writes in detail about her awakening love for him.

Otto pushed Margot and Anne to study hard; of course he didn't want them to be behind when they could go back to school. But outside the hours for homework and chores, Anne had time and complete freedom to write everything in her diary that she found important. She also wrote stories based on events in the Annex, and sometimes she read them to the others.

After she had been writing for about two years, something happened that influenced her writing dramatically. On March 28, 1944, as they did almost every evening, the group in hiding listened to Radio Orange, the broadcasting station in London of the Dutch government in exile. The speaker was the minister of education, art, and science, Gerrit Bolkestein (1871–1956), a liberal democrat, who talked about the situation to be expected after the war and the fact that the occupation period should be recorded. Anne writes: "Mr. Bolkestein, the Cabinet Minister, speaking on the Dutch broadcast from London, said that after the war a collection would be made of diaries and letters dealing with the war. Of course everyone pounced on my diary. Just imagine how interesting it would be if I were to publish a novel about the Secret Annex. The title alone would make people think that it was a detective novel" (March 29, 1944).

Anne, who had written earlier that she wanted to be a journalist, must have considered this appeal from London as a challenge. A few weeks later, on May 11, 1944, she wrote: "In any case, after the war I'd like to publish a book called *The Secret Annex*. It remains to be seen whether I'll succeed, but my diary can serve as the basis."

Anne started to rewrite her diary on loose sheets of carbon paper. This became the second version of her diary, in which she left out some matters, expanded others, and sometimes changed the dates. She also drew up a list with pseudonyms: The Van Pels family became Van Daan, and Pfeffer became Dussel. She even changed the name Frank to Robin. While she was working on her second version, she continued to write her first one, a double effort. Early in August 1944, she had completed the rewriting to the end of March 1944.

The End

The end came after twenty-five months of hiding. On Friday, August 4, 1944, an arresting squad of the *Sicherheitsdienst* (SD) burst in, led by Karl Silberbauer (1911–1972), a noncommissioned officer who was originally from Vienna. The other policemen were Dutch. From the beginning it was clear that there must have been a betrayal, for the squad knew that Jews were hidden in the Annex. However, they were amazed that there were so many people and had to call for a larger car. Silberbauer was surprised when he found out that Otto Frank had been an officer in the German army in the First World War. There was no longer any talk about hurrying, and he even explained that it would have been better if Otto Frank had reported for the Theresienstadt concentration camp because, as a former German officer, he would have been privileged over "ordinary" Jews.

After a few nights in the prison on Weteringschans, the eight Jews were transported to Westerbork. During this time, Miep Gies tried to free them. As a fellow townswoman from Vienna, she tried to soften up Silberbauer and even collected some money to try to bribe him. Her efforts were in vain; the eight residents from the Annex remained in Westerbork for a month, and from there they were deported to Auschwitz on September 3. This last transport from the Netherlands to the death camps consisted of 498 men, 442 women, and 79 children; a third of this group was gassed upon arrival. The only one of the eight from the Annex to survive was Otto Frank. The others died on different dates and in various camps—Margot and Anne, between late March and early April 1945 in concentration camp Bergen-Belsen. They lie there in one of the mass graves. On January 27, 1945, Auschwitz was liberated by the Russians; the only reason Otto survived was because he was in the hospital when the Germans retreated. In March he wrote a letter from Poland to his second cousin Milly Stanfield in Great Britain: "We are now waiting for repatriation, but it's still war and we are far from home. The Netherlands are still partially occupied. I know nothing about Edith and the children. We were separated upon our arrival at Birkenau-Auschwitz on September 5."

Otto Frank was part of a group of survivors who left by train in a south-eastern direction, to the port of Odessa on the Black Sea. En route Otto renewed his acquaintance with Elfriede Geiringer-Markovits (1905–1998) and her daughter, Eva, who was Anne's age. They knew each other from Amsterdam. Elfriede and Eva had survived Auschwitz, but not her husband or their son. Eight years later, Otto Frank and Elfriede Markovits were married.

From Odessa, Otto was taken to the south of France on the Monoway, a New Zealand ship, and arrived in Marseille on May 27, 1945. On June 3, he reached Amsterdam and went to Miep and Jan Gies, with whom he stayed for a considerable time. At this time he found out that his wife, Edith, had died, but he was still hopeful about the fate of his two daughters. Early in August, he received definite confirmation of their deaths. At that point Miep handed him Anne's diaries. Miep had picked up the diaries and the loose sheets that were lying in a heap and had taken them to safety before the furniture was removed from the Annex by a Dutch company under German orders. Miep said that she'd never looked at them and had saved them for their author, Anne.

The Betrayal

In addition to Otto having to rebuild his life and his company, he was preoccupied by the question of who had betrayed those hidden in the Annex. At first, the suspicion fell on Willem van Maaren (1895–1991), who worked in the warehouse. The hidden residents had been afraid of him; sometimes he behaved suspiciously, and on September 16, 1943, Anne wrote about him: "We wouldn't care what Mr. van Maaren thought of the situation except that he's known to be unreliable and to possess a high degree of curiosity. He's not one who can be put off with a flimsy excuse." The Political Investigation Department (PRA) of the Amsterdam police started an investigation of Van Maaren. The PRA was engaged in tracking down people who had helped the enemy during the war, and this included betrayals. The PRA concluded: "The suspect denies the betrayal, and the evidence is very vague. Accordingly, there is no case to answer." The discharge was conditional; he had to be monitored by the Supervisory Board for Political Offenders and lost his right to vote and stand for election for ten years. Van Maaren found this unacceptable and appealed; he was cleared on August 13, 1949, and all actions against him were dropped.

Fourteen years later, the Department of Justice was again interested in Van Maaren. The identity of Silberbauer had become known in October 1963, and since the diary of Anne Frank had become world famous, the betrayal became important once again. Van Maaren's movements were checked once more, but this time more carefully. However, nothing detrimental was found except for the fact that he was called "financially unreliable." The case against Van Maaren was closed; in *De Dagboeken van Anne Frank*, published in 1986, these two investigations are examined in detail.

There was nothing new until 1998, when the first serious biography of Anne Frank was published; it was written by Melissa Müller, an Austrian journalist. She tried to find the person who betrayed those in hiding. Starting from the story that a woman had called the *Sicherheitsdienst* to tell them that Jews were hidden at 263 Prinsengracht, Müller settled on Lena Hartog-van Bladeren as the likely culprit. Her husband worked in the warehouse, and she was afraid that he would be in danger if the Germans accidentally found the Jews. This story is not logical; first of all, there is no proof that she knew about the hidden Jews, and second, it's odd that her husband was at work as usual on the day of the raid.

Is it possible that an insider betrayed those in hiding? And if so, who? There is another possible suspect, but we should state immediately that there is no criminal file on this person in the National Archives. Nellie Voskuijl (1923–2001), a sister of Bep Voskuijl, worked until at least mid-May 1944 at a German airfield near Laôn, northeast of Paris. On May 11, 1944, Anne wrote: "The radio has said more than once that certain people, girls as well as boys, women as well as men [who work for the enemy], will be punished after the war for treason." It's possible that Nellie knew that Jews were hidden, since her sister, Bep, was involved with them on a daily basis and her father had made the bookcase for the entrance door. After the war, nothing was done about it, not even about her "working for the enemy." In a 2015 biography of Bep Voskuijl, *Bep Voskuijl, het zwijgen voorbij* (No more silence), Nellie was named as a possible collaborator, but there is no proof at all.

In 2002 the British journalist Carol Ann Lee published *The Hidden Life of Otto Frank*, which caused a great deal of controversy, first of all because she wrote that Otto Frank's company did business with the *Wehrmacht*, meaning that he was actually an economic collaborator. She went still further by stating that pectin was even delivered to the headquarters of the

German army (OKW), but this assertion resulted from her poor knowledge of German. The pectin wasn't delivered to the headquarters of the German army; instead, the delivery conditions were determined by the headquarters—a perfectly understandable situation. More than ten years earlier, Miep Gies had written in *Anne Frank Remembered*: "Some of these orders [for pectin] came from German army camps in the country." Otto Frank's "collaboration" was important for Lee to support her betrayal theory.

Lee's story that Otto Frank had been blackmailed since April 1941 by Tonny Ahlers (1917–2000), a small-time criminal from Amsterdam who worked for the *Sicherheitsdienst*, among others, wasn't convincing either. Supposedly, he had disclosed the address on Prinsengracht and continued blackmailing Otto after the war with regard to the so-called collaboration. Hard evidence is lacking, and Ahlers's family members, in particular, are the ones who claim that he was the informer. The most important "proof" is a statement by Ahlers's son, who at the age of seven had overheard a telephone conversation in which his father had talked about his own treachery. Ahlers's son disclosed this story fifty years later.

Other potential informers appear in Lee's book, and this slightly undermines Ahlers's claim: the private night watchman, M. Slegers, who discovered a burglary in the front part of 263 Prinsengracht in April 1944; "someone from the Jewish Council"; Maarten Kuiper (1898–1948), a member of the SD; and Ans van Dijk (1905–1948) and Branca Simons (1918–1979), two Jewish traitors. After the war, Kuiper and Van Dijk were tried and executed as "Jew-hunters."

In 2003 Gerrold van der Stroom and this author published *Wie verraadde Anne Frank?* (Who betrayed Anne Frank?). In this study, we examined all the betrayal theories and found none of them believable. We checked on what could have happened, and two things struck us. First, a sea of windows on houses from the even side of Keizersgracht and Westermarkt can be seen from the Annex. Conversely, the Annex can be seen from all these windows, and hundreds of residents could have seen that something unusual was going on there. Second, it is evident from the diary that those in hiding were frequently careless, although they were quite aware that no one should ever hear or see them. On July 11, 1942, Anne wrote about it: "Whatever we do, we're very afraid the neighbors might hear or see us. We started off immediately the first day sewing curtains. Actually you can hardly call them that, since they're nothing but scraps of fabric, varying greatly in shape, quality and pattern, which Father and I stitched crookedly together with unskilled fingers. These works of art were tacked to the windows, where they'll stay until we come out of hiding."

This was also true for the side of the gardens in the back of the houses, and on November 28, 1942, Anne reported that, using binoculars, she looked into the lighted rooms of the backdoor neighbors: "During the day our curtains can't be opened, not even an inch, but there's no harm when it's so dark."

But those in hiding did come to the front of the house, for example, on Saturday afternoon for their weekly bath. The curtains were closed, and they took turns washing themselves, "while the one who isn't in the bath looks out the window through a chink in the curtains and gazes in wonder at the endlessly amusing people." The urge to look outside doesn't decrease, and on November 3, 1943, Anne writes, "Sometimes one of the ladies or gentlemen can't resist the urge to peek outside." After the reproaches, the answer was usually, "Oh, nobody will notice." In the spring of 1944, things went wrong again. On April 11 of that year, Anne writes: "Peter isn't allowed to open his window anymore, since one of the Keg people noticed it was open." (Keg was a wholesale tea and coffee-roasting company at 265 Prinsengracht.) This clearly happened more often, for one can read in Anne's diary on April 15, 1944: "The windows in the Annex were open, and the Keg people saw that too. What must they be thinking?" A few months later, Anne writes that she herself had gone downstairs one evening and "looked outside from the window of the private office and kitchen." Careless? No doubt, no matter how understandable it seems. In the diary more examples of careless behavior can be found, and this carelessness could have been an important factor in the betrayal.

It's possible that chance played a much greater role than has been assumed and that the assumption of a purposeful attempt to betray the Frank family and the others to the Germans may be less likely. Things may have gone as follows: One of the rear neighbors saw one or more hidden Jews and told this to a "good" Dutchman, who then told someone else, and so on, until at a certain point the Germans were informed by name or anonymously. Of the more than 25,000 Jews who were hidden in the Netherlands, around

8,000–9,000 fell into the hands of the Germans, usually by betrayal. After the war, only a fraction of these traitors were tracked down and tried.

Vogelvrij; De jacht op de Joodse onderduiker (Outlawed: Hunting for Jews in hiding) by the journalist Sytze van der Zee was published in 2010. This writer agrees with the authors of *Wie verraade Anne Frank?* (Who betrayed Anne Frank?) that Tonny Ahlers can't be the culprit, but he develops an old betrayal theory. He points to Ans van Dijk, executed in 1948, as the informant, but words like "probably," "it could be," "it would equally well be possible," and "another possibility" are used too often around the betrayal of Anne Frank, so this remains no more than a theoretical possibility.

Toward the end of 2016, the Anne Frank House reported that research had revealed that the raid was probably not carried out because the hidden Jews were betrayed. It was instead most likely part of an investigation into fraud with ration coupons. The arrest of Anne Frank and her fellow hidden Jews was most likely a "bycatch," incidental to the fraud investigation. Unfortunately, there is no evidence or any sources for this theory either.

In *The Diary of Anne Frank: The Revised Critical Edition*, the conclusion is as follows: "It is no longer possible to reconstruct exactly what happened." This will have to suffice for the time being.

2

Anne Frank: From Diary to *Het Achterhuis/ Das Tagebuch/Le Journal/The Diary*

"[I] KEEP TRYING TO FIND a way to become what I'd like to be and what I could be if . . . if only there were no other people in the world." Those were the last words that Anne wrote in her diary on August 1, 1944, three days before the raid directed by the Germans. On June 25, 1947, her father wrote "BOOK" in his pocket calendar.

In a little less than three years, Anne's wish to become a writer was granted posthumously.

What happened during these three years that caused an adolescent's diary entries to be turned into a book? A book that would conquer the world and make its author into an icon of the Holocaust. Almost everyone is familiar with the image of the square autograph album that is known as *The Diary of Anne Frank*. In December 1943, that album was almost filled. Anne continued writing in a school exercise book and then in another one in 1944. For the sake of convenience, these are called diary 1, 2, and 3. In addition, there were more than three hundred loose sheets, the partially copied and partially rewritten version of her diary. But Anne had written more. She wrote "favorite quotes," mostly short and longer quotes from world literature, in an office ledger. On the first page, she wrote: "One of Pim's inventions!" Pim was the nickname she used for her father, and it's likely that Otto encouraged her to copy beautiful or interesting quotes. It wasn't until 2004 that this part of Anne's effort to become a writer was published in its entirety. Anne also wrote "Stories and Sketches from the Annex" in a large notebook with a cardboard cover. She copied part of this in her diary, or she may have written it first in her diary and then put it in her "Book of Tales" (Verhaaltjesboek).

It's no longer possible to discover the exact order. Anne also wrote a few stories on the loose sheets.

Early in August 1945, Otto was notified that his two daughters had died. It was then that Miep Gies gave him all of Anne's diaries and other manuscripts. Of course, he knew that Anne, just like Margot, had kept a diary, but he had no idea of its contents. Anne had, from time to time, read a story to the group in hiding, but now her father could read everything she had written. He decided that something had to be done with her diaries. His relatives—for example, his mother in Basel—and his friends in Amsterdam had often asked him what life in hiding had been like. Now he was holding the answer. He used a typewriter to copy *das Wesentliche* (the essentials) of Anne's writings, leaving out what seemed uninteresting to him—like Anne's very critical comments about her mother. He spared people who were still alive as well as those who had died. These were, of course, edits based on his personal decisions, but the essentials were supposedly kept. Otto then translated it into German and sent it to his mother. Almost fifteen years later, he declared before an examining magistrate in Lübeck (see page 58) that his first typescript of the diaries had been lost.

Otto immediately set to work typing out the pages again, but this time he used the second version that Anne had written on the loose sheets. That was certainly in the spirit of Anne, who had started to rewrite her first version; her second version was written with an eye to publication. This time, Otto didn't copy everything from only the second version; he also used the "lost" first version. This was logical, since her rewritten version went only to the end of March 1944, and therefore he had to use the first version for the months of March to August 1944. In addition, he also copied four stories from Anne's "Book of Tales," and this is how a first typescript came into existence. Unlike the first copy, this typescript was not lost and is in the possession of the Frank family. In it, one can see clearly how Otto cut and pasted retyped sentences and entire passages. Once again, he left out things, but the structure remained untouched; it was a diary that ran from June 1942 to August 1944. The fact that there were dates that didn't tally can't be ascribed only to Otto Frank. Especially in her first diary, Anne had changed dates or pasted fragments of text in between her diary letters, sometimes making it unclear which passage belonged to which date.

But a typescript was not yet a book, and at this point, Otto Frank asked Albert Cauvern—the husband of Otto's former secretary, Isa Cauvern, and dramaturg at a Dutch radio station—to "revise" the manuscript. Years later, Otto explained what he meant: "to check it for grammatical errors and to remove Germanisms, that is, to remove expressions that my daughter had taken from the German language and which were therefore bad Dutch." That was sensible of Otto Frank, since Dutch was not his first language. Albert Cauvern started his work as editor and made numerous changes and corrections. In this way, a number of Germanisms were corrected, but in the typescript, there are also expansions of Anne's text. On July 6, 1944, Anne wrote in a passage about Peter: "It's hard enough standing on your own two feet, but when you also have to remain true to your own character and soul, it's harder still." Cauvern changed the sentence as follows: "It's hard enough standing on your own two feet for a type like Peter, but it's even harder to stand on your own feet as a conscious living human being." That doesn't seem to be a significant change, but it's not what Anne had written.

In regard to content, a significant edit was made the first time Anne mentions Pfeffer, who came to live in the Annex in November 1942: "a dentist named Fritz Pfeffer. He lives with a charming Christian lady who's quite a bit younger than he. They're probably not married, but that's beside the point." This was changed to "whose wife is fortunately living in a foreign country." The woman Anne referred to was Charlotte Kaletta (1920–1984); Otto Frank must have made this change because he knew her well, both before and after the war. At the time, living together without being married was something that people would rather not admit, and in this way Otto could protect Charlotte's reputation.

At this point, all the pseudonyms that Anne had made up were introduced, with one exception. As already mentioned briefly, Anne had chosen Robin instead of Frank as her last name. She indicated this on her list of names, but Frank remained Frank. With the adoption of all the changes, a new typescript was made, this time typed by Isa Cauvern, and copies were made. Otto gave these to friends and acquaintances, and we are familiar with the reactions of some of them. One example is that of Dr. Kurt Baschwitz (1886–1968), who had been part of the Franks' circle of acquaintances before the war. He had fled Germany in 1933. On February 10, 1946, Baschwitz wrote to his daughter:

I have just been reading the diary of Anne Frank, the youngest daughter of our friend Frank. You must have known her. They were, as you know, in hiding for 2 years. The girl, 14 and then 15 years old, kept a diary that escaped the Germans' notice as if by a miracle. It is the most moving document about this time that I know, and an astonishing literary masterpiece as well. It reveals the inner experiences of a maturing girl. Her impressions in close confinement with her father, whom she loved dearly, the mother, with whom she clashed, her sister, whom she discovered to be a friend, with the other family that shared their hiding place, and with their son with whom she began to fall in love. I think it ought to appear in print.

Otto Frank thought so too, but it wasn't easy. He contacted several publishers who showed no interest in the diary musings of an unknown Jewish girl. Nonetheless, Otto persisted and gave the manuscript to Dr. Werner Cahn, who had also fled Germany and was working for several publishers in the Netherlands. Cahn knew Annie Romein-Verschoor (1895–1978), a writer and historian, and her husband, Jan Romein (1893–1962), a professor of history at the University of Amsterdam. Annie Romein was impressed by the diary and approached several publishers, "but the certainty prevailed there at the time that interest in anything to do with the war was stone-dead." Her husband also read the manuscript and expressed his admiration in an article that appeared on the front page of the former resistance newspaper *Het Parool* on April 3, 1946.

By chance a diary written during the war years has come into my possession. The Netherlands Institute for War Documentation already possesses some two hundred similar diaries, but I should be very much surprised if there were another as lucid, as intelligent, and at the same time as natural. This one made me forget the present and its many calls to duty for a whole evening as I read it from beginning to end. When I finished it was nighttime and I was astonished to find that the lights still worked, that we still had bread and tea, that I could hear no airplanes droning overhead, and no pounding of army boots in the street—I had been so engrossed in my reading, so carried away back to that unreal world, now almost a year behind us.

To me however, this apparently inconsequential diary of a child, this *de profundis* stammered out in a child's voice, embodies all the hideousness of fascism, more so than all the evidence at Nuremberg put together. To me the fate of this Jewish girl epitomizes the worst crime perpetrated by everlastingly abominable minds. For the worst crime is not the destruction of life and culture as such—these could also fall victim to a culture-creating revolution—but the throttling of the sources of culture, the destruction of life and talent for the mere sake of mindless destructiveness.

Het Achterhuis

Various publishers now started to show interest, and it was publishing house Contact that risked publishing the diary. Contact was established in 1933, had obvious antifascist publications on its list, and for years published the successful series *De schoonheid van ons land* (The beauty of our country). The publisher was quite progressive in publishing *Het sexueele leven van den mensch* (The sexual life of human beings), which had many printings starting in 1937 and was designated as a forbidden book by Roman Catholic newspapers. That's why it's strange that Director G. P. de Neve objected to the publication of *Het Achterhuis* because of certain passages—for example, the one about Anne's menstruation. People involved with the publisher as well as Miep and Jan Gies later recounted that De Neve was a devout Catholic and had even talked with his priest about the publication. De Neve's behavior is hardly in keeping with the prewar sex education book or with the fact that he is recorded as belonging to "no religious denomination" in the Amsterdam municipal register.

In some passages, it is obvious that Anne herself didn't copy certain matters she had written in her first version into her second version. On October 3, 1942, she writes about Eva's period (*Eva's Youth* by Nico van Suchtelen) and sighs, "Oh, I long to get my period—then I'll really be grown up." Anne didn't copy this in her second version, but Otto did copy it in the final typescript. More than a year later, when she discusses the sex life of cats and, in particular, of their cat Mouschi with Peter, she writes: "The female one is a vagina, that I know, but I don't know what it's called in males" (January 24, 1944). Anne didn't copy this in her rewritten version either, but Otto Frank used it anyway.

There is one clear example of intervention by the publisher. It concerns a passage in which Anne describes how in the past she spent the night with her girlfriend Jacque and was curious about her body: "I asked her whether, as proof our friendship, we could touch each other's breasts. Jacque refused" (January 5, 1944). Anne didn't copy this in her second version, and it's not in the 1947 printed version. Remarkably, this deleted section did appear in the 1950 translation, thanks to Otto Frank. He clearly disagreed with these and other deletions and sent them to the English publisher and the translator. According to his enclosed letter, these were passages "which were not printed in the Dutch edition because they were either too long or were likely to offend Dutch Puritan or Catholic susceptibilities. [...] and wonder if you would be so good as to translate them for us." The English translation is therefore slightly more extensive than the original Dutch publication.

In any case, Otto Frank was the one who had to give his consent for the final version. There were various discussions, as evident from a letter dated October 19, 1946, from Otto Frank to the Contact publishing house: "I have your letter of this month and am writing to inform you that I would like to discuss the proposed deletions with you. I agree with part of them without any problem, whereas there is a difference of opinion about other things." This might refer to the undated note "Proposed deletions." There were twenty-six; sixteen of them were carried out, in addition to numerous small deletions that were mostly grammatical in nature.

Every publisher tinkers with manuscripts, some more than others, and this is what happened to Anne Frank's manuscript. Contact had its own guidelines, and the book had to conform to the size of books of the Prologue series of new writers. In reality, there would be ten extra pages, in addition to photos of Anne, the hinged bookcase, her handwriting, and a floor plan of the house at 263 Prinsengracht. No one paid much attention to this; however, doubts were raised later, primarily by neo-Nazis, about the authenticity of the diary, and any change made by a publisher or someone else was seized upon as "proof." It turned out to be difficult to figure out who had done what because ordinary editing had now landed in the public arena.

While the editors at Contact were busy getting the manuscript ready for publication, a prepublication of five "Fragments from the Diary of Anne Frank" appeared in a new literary magazine, *De Nieuwe Stem* (The new voice). The short introduction stated that Anne Frank had been in hiding with her parents and her sister, but that she and her family had been arrested and deported. "The diary was saved by chance." Nothing about her death or her father's survival was mentioned. Otto Frank and Werner Cahn were responsible for this publication. It shows that Otto took the publication of his daughter's work seriously and did not neglect the commercial side. He changed the standard contract with the publisher so that he kept the translation, stage, and film rights himself. At the time, it was probably of little importance to the publisher.

In the summer of 1947, the book was published: *Het Achterhuis. Diary Entries from June 12, 1942—August 1, 1944.* At Otto Frank's request, there was a foreword by Annie Romein-Verschoor, in which she emphasized Anne's candor and her "accelerated development to adulthood":

> There is more to say about this diary. It is a war document, a record of the cruelty and dismal suffering of the Jews' persecution, of human helpfulness and betrayal, of human adaptation and non-adaptation; the small joys and the great and small miseries of life in hiding are described in a direct, un-literary and therefore an often excellent way by this child that had at least one important quality of a great writer: remaining candid, not getting used to—hence becoming blind to—the things as they are. [. . .] Just like that brave little geranium that blossomed and kept blossoming behind the blacked-out windows of the Annex.

On the book flap there was a part of Jan Romein's article in *Het Parool*, but that was a one-off, since Romein objected because permission had not been requested to reprint it. A short epilogue described what had happened to those in hiding and their helpers, and there was a reassuring sentence about the publication: "The original text has been printed except for a few passages that are of little importance to the reader." Everyone involved with the publication must have realized this was far from the truth. This was especially true for Otto Frank, the person ultimately responsible for the book's publication. The first printing was a little more than three thousand copies, but before the end of the year there was already a second printing. Two more printings were required the following year, then one in 1949 and another one in 1950. The next printing wasn't until 1953, but there were another three printings that year alone. This was quite a success for an unknown writer— the positive reviews must have helped.

Jacques Presser, a historian who had taught at the Jewish High School in Amsterdam, wrote that after liberation he had read very little that was "so pure, so moving" as Anne's diary. After examining the probable betrayal, he concluded that everyone would love Anne Frank and that she had won everyone's hearts with her diary. In this way, she also urged "us, those left

behind and the survivors, to transcend our anger and bitterness with something that is more, and can be more, than sorrow and resignation."

The theater critic Jeanne van Schaik-Willing wrote in a weekly magazine (*De Groene Amsterdammer*): "Now that her lot was as bitter as it was,
Anne Frank not only created the self-portrait of the budding young woman,
but she also became the symbol of the lot of her kind, who were murdered
by the Germans." Neither the word "Jew" nor the phrase "persecution of
Jews" appeared in this article. A review in a socialist weekly (*De Vlam*)
ended as follows: "Parents and educators are advised urgently to read this
book." In a daily paper (*NRC*), the writer, Anna Blaman, wrote that readers had quickly become fed up with war literature because of the "often low
literary level of the writings in question." But if such a war document was
also a "document humain," then it's another story. That was true for Anne's
diary, and Blaman had "respect for the nobility of this innocent human soul
deprived of its right to exist and respect for the quiet heroism with which
this human soul tried to endure the outrageous assault in her right to exist." The fact that Anne was Jewish was not mentioned. In a detailed review
in the Jewish weekly (*Nieuw Israëlitisch Weekblad*), the author, Jaap Meijer,
called Anne "a typical Jewish child from a typical emigrant milieu." Meijer
felt that these emigrants "haven't found their way to their own people" and
that "any Jewish orientation was totally lacking." According to Meijer, this
was reflected in the diary: "Prayer, which is mentioned from time to time,
evokes a vague notion of Christian humanism. There is a growing distance
from Jews, who (typical of this innocent child) are simply identified with
'poor people.'"

Anne's "Jewishness"—touched on by Meijer—emerged more intensely
ten years later after the American stage adaptation of the diary. Meanwhile,
Otto Frank kept a close eye on Contact to make sure that a new printing
would be published in time, and he managed to persuade the publisher to
publish *Do You Remember? Stories and Fairytales,* which included eight stories by Anne, in 1949. It was illustrated with drawings by Kees Kelfkens,
and the afterword was written by Anne Winkler-Vonk, a children's book author. She wrote carefully about "these laboriously produced brainchildren,"
saying, "It is not proper for us to criticize these creations." Annie Romein-
Verschoor wrote sternly about "a negligible bundle of immature children's
stories." When Anne's *Verhaaltjesboek* (Book of tales) was published in 1960,

there were similar reactions. The weekly magazine *Vrij Nederland* wrote: "Anne Frank cult, shopping lists are revealing, but fatal for a saint."

Das Tagebuch

Otto Frank didn't sit still; in looking for a German translator, he found Anneliese Schütz, who had also come to the Netherlands as a Jewish refugee before the war and was part of the Frank family's circle of friends. She had worked as a journalist in Berlin but had never done translations. Schütz didn't translate from *Het Achterhuis* but from the second typescript, so *Das Tagebuch* differed from *Het Achterhuis*. The previously mentioned Werner Cahn said that it was a correct translation to be sure, but it "did not always reflect the style of the young Anne Frank. . . . and this may well be the reason why in well-intentioned German literary circles doubts were expressed occasionally about the authenticity of the diary." Later, Otto Frank would also concede that Mrs. Schütz had been "too old" to make this translation: "Many of her expressions were pedantic and not in a youthful enough style. In addition she [. . .] misunderstood many Dutch expressions."

One could call these technical problems in the translation, since the translator, who was over fifty, had the difficult task of rendering the Dutch of a thirteen- to fourteen-year-old-girl into German. The language became a somewhat formal German in which all of Anne's natural gracefulness had disappeared. However, the political changes introduced in this translation are much more interesting. This concerns anti-German passages that were omitted or had been made more inoffensive. When the dentist joined the group of the residents in hiding, he was presented with a copy of the "Annex Hiding Rules" that included the following: "Only the language of civilized people may be spoken, therefore no German." The translator changed it to: "All civilized languages . . . but softly" (*Alle Kultursprache . . . aber leise*). Anne's remark, "And there is no greater hostility in the world than exists between Germans and Jews," was toned down to "And there is no greater hostility in the world than between these Germans and the Jews" (*Und eine grössere Feindschaft als zwischen diesen Deutschen und den Juden gibt es nicht auf der Welt*). Anne's "heroism in the war or when confronting the Germans" became "heroism in the war or against oppression" (*Heldenmut im Krieg und im Streit gegen Unterdrückung*). Otto Frank agreed to this translation, but he tried later to blame the German publisher for a number of these "political" changes. However, it is much more likely that Anneliese Schütz was right when almost ten years later she wrote in *Der Spiegel* that "a book intended after all for sale in Germany [. . .] cannot contain invectives against the Germans." It is no longer possible to ascertain whether it was Otto Frank, the publisher, or the translator who first suggested these changes, but it's a fact that all three parties approved them. It would not be the last time that Otto Frank compromised in order to sell his daughter's ideals.

Lambert Schneider, a publisher in Heidelberg, released the book with the title *Das Tagebuch der Anne Frank* in a printing of forty-five hundred copies in 1950. Marie Baum, a German social work educator who had turned actively against the Nazis, wrote in the foreword, which definitely had a political overtone: "Once again we are burdened in a terrible way by the unredeemable culpability of the persecution of the Jews." And she referred to Germans as "perpetrators."

Five years later, Fischer Bücherei published a paperback edition; its foreword, written by Albrecht Goes, an author and a Protestant theologian, was more neutral and apolitical:

The only thing that remains for us is this diary—one of the most remarkable documents of an awakening human being, written down absolutely without any ulterior motives and because of that perfectly pure . . .

In conclusion we should note that this discussion on these pages between the I and the world is carried out with an uncommon determination. This young person who can love and hate, fight and suffer, knows to which aim her way must lead, which answer is being asked of her, for the sake of the hour, for the sake of the people—of the people that for Anne is called the Netherlands—and Israel.

In Goes's foreword, there is no mention of the persecution of the Jews; only "Israel" is mentioned.

In this paperback, two "tales" are included that were missing in the earlier German edition and also in *Het Achterhuis*. Therefore, German readers had a poor translation but more text by Anne Frank. Otto Frank had sent these tales to Fischer Verlag.

For a long time, Anne's father had resisted an East German edition, but after the play was staged in that country, he changed his mind. Finally, in the fall of 1957, the book appeared in the GDR (German Democratic Republic) with the same foreword by Goes.

Le Journal

In 1950 a French translation, *Le Journal d'Anne Frank,* was published by Calmann-Levy, and it seems that the translators, T. Caren and Suzanne Lombard, used the Contact edition, for there do not appear to be any differences when compared to the Dutch edition. The foreword was by Daniel-Rops, a Catholic author, who toyed seriously with fascism before the war but changed his mind just in time. Annie Romein-Verschoor remarked bitterly, but not entirely correctly, that the French edition now had to be adorned "with a foreword by a collaborator, and one assumed in addition that a collaborator was also an anti-Semite, who dunked the Anne Frank myth in a Christian sugar syrup." In his foreword, Daniel-Rops remarked that an adult writer had perhaps worked on it, but he quickly pushed that aside: "Anne Frank's daily entries are so pure in tone, so true, that the thought wouldn't enter anyone's head that she would have written them with the intention of making *literature,* and even less that some adult would have corrected it. From beginning to end one gets the impression of undisputed authenticity. If the word didn't have a dusty and faded connotation, one would say that it's a document."

The Diary

The step to English, the most widely used language in the world, still had to take place, and here, too, Otto Frank was active. Later, various people would maintain that they had been responsible for the English-language edition. One of them was the American novelist Meyer Levin (1906–1981), who for more than ten years was to play a notable and controversial role in the continuing history of Anne's diary. As the son of Jewish emigrants from Russia, he grew up in a poor Jewish area of Chicago. At the end of the Second World War, he was a European correspondent for the Overseas News Agency and reported the horrors of concentration camps like Dachau and Buchenwald. These experiences caused him to become a confirmed Zionist. Levin worked as a journalist, wrote many novels, and also made some movies. He would constantly have doubts about his talent and the place of the Jews in the Diaspora. From 1950 to 1951, Levin lived in France with his wife, Tereska Torrès. In her book, *Les maisons hantées de Meyer Levin* (The haunted houses of Meyer Levin), she claims that she bought the French translation of *Het Achterhuis* in Antibes in the summer of 1951. The date she mentions is difficult to reconcile with the fact that Levin had already mentioned Anne's diary in a review of Hershey's *The Wall* in the Jewish magazine *Congress Weekly* of November 1950. Levin also writes that he had contacted Otto Frank, who told him that "the book had been refused by a number of important American publishers." An editor of the famous publisher Alfred A. Knopf described Anne's diary as "a gloomy account of family squabbles, petty annoyances, and adolescent emotions."

Eventually, an American publisher was willing to publish the diary on the condition that a British publisher would participate and share the translating and printing costs. The British publisher, Valentine, Mitchell & Co Ltd., asked Mrs. B. M. Mooyaard-Doubleday (no relation of the publisher), who lived in the Netherlands, to translate *Het Achterhuis*. For her translation, she used the fourth or fifth printing of *Het Achterhuis*. At the request of the publisher, but actually at the request of Otto Frank, some passages were included that had not made it into the Dutch edition. This involved seven passages, including the already mentioned passage about touching breasts and one about menstruation, as well as one about Frans Liszt, who was "the greatest womanizer, even at the age of seventy. He had an affair with Countess Marie d'Agoult, Princesse Carolyne Sayn-Wittgenstein, the dancer Lola Montez, the pianist Agnes Kingworth, the pianist Sophie Menter, the Circassian princess Olga Janina, Baroness Olga Meyendorff, actress Lilla what's her name, etc., etc., and there's no end to it." Evidently, this was not acceptable in the puritanical Netherlands, but it was no problem in Great Britain and the United States.

The British-American translation with the title *Anne Frank: The Diary of a Young Girl* was published in 1952, and the American Doubleday edition contained a foreword by Eleanor Roosevelt (1884–1962). This wasn't the only foreword ever written by the president's widow (and in this case probably written by Barbara Zimmerman Epstein, the editor of the book), but it indicated that the publisher and Eleanor Roosevelt thought it was an important book. The foreword stated, "Reading it is a rich and rewarding experience," and the sentence, "One of the wisest and most moving commentaries on war and its impact on human beings that I have ever read," was later used innumerable times as advertising for the book.

The first printing consisted of a modest five thousand copies, and there was no advertising. Meyer Levin succeeded in getting a favorable review published in the *New York Times Book Review*. "Anne Frank's voice becomes the voice of six million vanished souls" was on the front page of this influential book review. In a second review, in *The National Jewish Post*, Levin insisted that a play and a movie should be made of the book. The *New York Times* review, in particular, seemed to create a demand for the book: A second printing with fifteen thousand copies quickly followed, and a few days later, a third printing of forty-five thousand copies. Numerous newspapers wanted to publish the book in serial form, and people agreed that Levin's review had been very important for this success.

Over the course of six years, *Het Achterhuis* and three important translations had been published, and the reviews were generally favorable. No one wondered whether it was literally Anne's diary, and Otto Frank never explained how *Het Achterhuis* had actually come about. Of course, no one looked at the various translations—not at the German, slightly dated and with some political censorship, or the English one that contained more than the Dutch original. A series of attacks on the authenticity of the diary— that continue to the present—started ten years after the publication of *Het Achterhuis* with an article in a Swedish neo-Nazi weekly, which asserted that Anne Frank was not the author (see page 56).

De Dagboeken van Anne Frank (The Diaries of Anne Frank)

When the critical edition of the diary, *De Dagboeken van Anne Frank*, was published in 1986 by the RIOD, predecessor of the NIOD, it was the first time that what had happened between 1942 and 1947 was clearly explained. In *De Dagboeken van Anne Frank*, the first version of Anne's diary, her second version, and *Het Achterhuis* were presented in a way that the reader could follow the development from manuscript to book.

Anne's own changes, deletions, and other alterations were made clearly visible, and it is also possible to see what Otto Frank and the publisher had done. The publication was chosen as one of the forty "most carefully edited books" of 1986. Among other things, the jury report said: "The quality of this book is to be found in the way in which editorial conception and the choice of form are inextricably connected. And it proves incidentally that a critical edition of a text doesn't have to be dull." This edition did not come about without problems, for there were people who felt that NIOD shouldn't touch the diaries. A member of Parliament, Wessel-Tuinstra, wondered whether it was correct to include diary fragments that Otto Frank had knowingly left out. She therefore asked A. Pais, the minister of education, to block this publication, but Pais didn't agree. He considered the intended publication "also as a tribute to Anne Frank and the more than one million other Jewish children who were murdered during the Second World War." Pais wanted an unabridged publication, whereby certain of Anne's remarks could be left out so that "the personal privacy of those involved would be sufficiently guaranteed." This meant that the NIOD had to ask permission of those persons mentioned by Anne in her diary, if they were still alive. It turned out that some had objections, and others did not. The Anne Frank Foundation, as the copyright holder, retained its right not to include certain passages. In the critical edition, these omissions are explained by footnotes. Moreover, the new Dutch publisher, no longer Contact but Bert Bakker, had to agree to this stipulation. Fortunately, the publisher agreed, and after extensive legal negotiations and complicated contracts between the NIOD, Bert Bakker, and the Anne Frank Foundation, work could get started. At an earlier stage, the Anne Frank House had revealed that it also wanted to make a critical edition. All parties thought it would be better if the Anne Frank Foundation and the Anne Frank House, with their significant business interests in the diary, would not be involved with anything regarding content. It wasn't until a few days before the publication of *De Dagboeken van Anne Frank* that they saw the content.

A reason to publish all the diary texts was that from the mid-fifties onward the authenticity of Anne's diary was continually called into question. This was also why the Netherlands Forensic Institute was involved. It was H. J. J. Hardy, in particular, who carried out extensive research into Anne Frank's handwriting; his colleagues examined the paper, the ink, and even the cover of Anne's first diary. The results of this research were detailed in a 270-page report. The conclusion was that "with a probability bordering on certainty," the diaries had been written by Anne Frank. In layman's language, the diary was authentic.

In the critical edition, seven introductory chapters covered the history of the Frank family, the time in hiding, the betrayal, the arrest, how *Het Achterhuis* and the play came about, an overview of the attacks on the diary's authenticity, and the research into handwriting identification and scientific document examination, presented in a shortened form.

Het Achterhuis, the New "Edition for General Readers"

The critical edition was translated into English, German, French, Japanese, and Italian, and a total of one hundred thousand copies were sold, which is unusual for a scholarly book. The Foundation in Basel, Otto Frank's heir, felt that it was time for a "new" Achterhuis. Much more was known about what Anne had written, and it would be easier to attune the translations of this "definitive" edition more closely to one another. Otto Frank's edition was adopted unabbreviated and supplemented with other passages from Anne's first and second versions. The new 1991 text is one-fourth more extensive "and is intended to give the reader a deeper insight into the world of Anne Frank." The foreword of the new "edition for general readers" states that Anne's text has been adapted to present-day spelling, spelling and linguistic errors have been corrected, and Germanisms that are no longer understandable have been replaced by contemporary Dutch. The foreword concludes as follows: "In our conviction that any additional alteration would only affect the authenticity of the diaries, we have left the rest of the text undisturbed." This short text is basically just as misleading as the one that has, since 1947, stood at the end of Het Achterhuis: "The original text has been printed, except for a few passages that are of little significance to the reader."

The most important argument for a new edition was not the deeper insight into the world of Anne Frank, but commerce, for copyrights expire seventy years after the death of the author. This would mean that seventy years after Anne Frank's death, Het Achterhuis would be in the public domain. Everyone would be able to publish it without having to pay anything to the Anne Frank Foundation. That is why the "definitive edition" came on the market in 1991, compiled by Miriam Pressler, the German translator of the critical edition, De Dagboeken van Anne Frank. The idea of the copyright holder, the Foundation, was that the new edition's copyrights wouldn't expire until seventy years after the death of Miriam Pressler, the compiler. It remains strange that an originally Dutch book, based on Dutch texts, is "augmented and updated" via a German detour. Actually, there is a question about whether the copyright can be extended in this way: Anne Frank is and remains the author of the original text, and 2015 was seventy years since her death.

Creation of an Image by the Book

During the first ten years after the original publication, the image of Anne was determined exclusively by the contents of *Het Achterhuis*—there was no Anne Frank House, and Anne was not yet claimed by anyone. A troublesome factor with *Het Achterhuis* is that most readers blindly assume that truth can be found in a diary or in diary letters. Or people believe that such a personal document reflects the thoughts and ideas of the writer in his or her entirety. But why couldn't there be untruths in such a document? And why couldn't other people's ideas or imaginings be written in it? On November 19, 1942, Anne wrote: "In the evenings when it's dark, I often see long lines of good, innocent people, accompanied by crying children, walking on and on, ordered about by a handful of men who bully and beat them until they nearly drop. No one is spared. The sick, the elderly, children, babies and pregnant women—all are marched to their death."

Many readers assume implicitly that Anne really saw this, and that's why this passage is often quoted. But we don't know if Anne actually wrote it on that date, for no first version is known to exist. In addition, in George Stevens's 1959 movie, there is a scene during which all those in hiding look outside at a group of Jews who are being led away by the Germans. The fact that this scene is obviously taking place in Staalstraat and was therefore impossible to see from Prinsengracht was probably noticed only by a Dutch audience. Prinsengracht was not the scene of roundups as described by Anne. Anne didn't see it and couldn't have seen it. She heard about roundups, for example, from the dentist Pfeffer (Dussel) who joined them in hiding on November 12, 1942. And there were few readers who realized that the afterword of *Het Achterhuis*, "The original text has been printed, except for a few passages that are of little significance to the reader" didn't correspond to reality. The fact that Anne had rewritten her diary became public knowledge in 1986 when *De Dagboeken van Anne Frank,* the critical edition, was published. And it wasn't until the "new" *Achterhuis* was published in 1991 that the existence of two diaries was mentioned for the first time in the foreword.

◇ **3** ◇

Anne Frank on Broadway: The Play

A RADIO DRAMA ABOUT ANNE Frank, written by Meyer Levin, was broadcast by CBS on September 14, 1952. Two months later, Anne's diary was broadcast in a dramatized form on television by NBC. Both broadcasts were most likely presented without Otto Frank's knowledge, let alone his permission.

Partly because Levin had convinced Otto Frank that he was responsible for the success of the English-language publication, Otto empowered him to act as his literary agent to create an American stage adaptation. Later, those involved would give another explanation for this agreement: Levin remained convinced that he had received firm permission from Otto Frank, while Otto kept talking about an "intention." Meanwhile, the increasing popularity of the book led to the call for a stage adaptation. Levin wanted to be more than a literary agent—he wanted to write the play himself. Eventually, Otto Frank yielded to this wish. Due in part to Doubleday's involvement, supported by Levin, Otto Frank chose the theater producer, Cheryl Crawford. She agreed to produce the play to be written by Levin on the condition that his adaptation was usable. She thought his first sketch was good and reported that to Otto Frank. Levin then started to work on the play and eventually gave his adaptation to Otto.

Almost forty years later, Tereska Torrès, Levin's wife, wrote in her book, *Les Maisons hantées de Meyer Levin* (The haunted houses of Meyer Levin):

The next day Otto Frank has Cheryl Crawford read the play, and her answer was not long in coming.

Meyer is so dismayed that at first he doesn't react. He is still pale when he states:

- She doesn't like my play at all.
- But that's impossible, Meyer, why, how?
- I don't know. I don't understand. She asked Lillian Hellmann's opinion, and she thought it was unplayable. She said "unplayable."
- Lillian Hellman, who is that?
- She is the best known female playwright in the United States and has just been summoned to appear before Senator McCarthy's committee, but she refused to name her Communist friends. She is the heroine of left-wing America.
  McCarthy, left-wing America, the producer, a famous playwright, and Meyer standing there, pale, looking stunned.
- What will you do now?
- I'll discuss it with Otto Frank. He'll defend me. He'll break the contract. After all, I recommended that producer because she agreed that I could write the play. If Otto has to choose between her and me, he has to choose me. I've been helping him to get the book published in the United States for two years.

The Play

Levin continued to insist that his adaptation should be performed, and he succeeded in persuading Otto Frank to select Kermit Bloomgarden as the producer instead of Cheryl Crawford. Bloomgarden had made a name for himself with productions of Arthur Miller's, among others. Unfortunately for Levin, however, Bloomgarden also rejected his play. Meanwhile, Otto had enlisted the legal help of the New York law firm Weiss, Rifkind, Wharton, and Garrison. To end the stalemate, a seemingly solid agreement was reached between Meyer Levin and Otto Frank. Levin would submit his version for approval to fourteen theater producers mentioned by name. If all fourteen rejected his version, he would reconcile himself to their verdict. The last article of the agreement was that Levin would no longer act as literary agent. Not one of the fourteen theater producers who were approached reacted favorably, and according to the agreement, Otto Frank was now rid of Meyer Levin. It turned out that nothing was further from the truth.

Bloomgarden now had carte blanche, and at the end of 1953, he asked the couple Frances Goodrich (1890–1984) and Albert Hackett (1900–1995) to make a stage adaptation. Frances Goodrich had been an actress and had written a number of plays with Albert Hackett, her third husband, who had also been an actor. Frances had an interesting link with the Netherlands: she had been married to Hendrik Willem van Loon (1882–1944), who was born in Rotterdam. After immigrating to the United States, he became a very successful author of popular historical books. In addition to plays, Goodrich and Hackett had written a large number of screenplays for Paramount and MGM. Three of them were based on stories by Dashiell Hammett, the popular writer of hard-boiled detective novels and longtime partner of Lillian Hellman. At an earlier stage, Hellman had been mentioned as the writer of the stage adaptation of Anne's diary, but in the end, she played only a consulting role. However, she was one of the investors in the play and profited from it.

When Bloomgarden approached Goodrich and Hackett, they were working at MGM, but they were granted a leave to write the play. Otto Frank was at first reluctant about letting "Hollywood writers" adapt his daughter's diary, but in the end, he approved. He immediately started to interfere with the content, telling the Hacketts not to concentrate on the Jewish aspect. Anne's ideas and ideals were universal and had to be highlighted to show humanity the consequences of discrimination, hate, and persecution. Otto wrote that Pfeffer the dentist had been a rather Orthodox Jew (unmarried and living with a Christian girlfriend?), while Otto's wife, Edith, was more liberal but had a deep religious faith, and Margot had followed in that direction. He himself had not been raised religiously, but after the experiences of the war, he had become more conscious of being Jewish. According to Otto, Anne was more inscrutable, but she cared little about outward religious appearances.

The stage adaptation turned out to be difficult, especially letting the eight people in hiding be "visible" during the entire play. Eight versions were needed before all parties, including Otto Frank, were satisfied with the result. To experience the atmosphere, the Hacketts and Garson Kanin, the proposed director, visited Amsterdam so that Otto could show them around the Annex. In addition, the photographer Maria Austria filmed the entire interior for them. They also spoke with Louis de Jong, the director of the NIOD.

After a preview performance in Philadelphia, the play opened in the Cort Theatre in New York on October 5, 1955. The Second World War had ended ten years earlier, but the fear of a third world war was still present, considering the warning in the program: "If there is an air raid alarm, stay in your seat and wait for the management's instructions." Both the stage-Otto (Joseph Schildkraut) as well as the stage-Edith (Gusti Huber) were born in Vienna. Meyer Levin later said that Huber had continued performing during the Nazi era and therefore had cooperated with the Nazis. Anne was played by seventeen-year-old Susan Strasberg, the daughter of Lee and Paula Strasberg, the founders of the famous Actors Studio. It was her debut. The performance was a great success with more than seven hundred Broadway performances, and the play received reviews ranging from good to very good.

The *New York Times* headline was "Lovely Drama Staged from Girl's Book," and the review ended as follows: "Out of the truth of a human being has come a delicate, rueful, moving drama."

Some excerpts from other reviews read as follows: "Stark Study of Terror, Skilled Cast Combines to Offer Powerful Evening in the Theatre"; "Diary of Anne Frank A Gripping Drama"; "Play based on a young girl's observation of Gestapo persecution and its impact"; and "As Mr. Frank, Mr. Schildkraut is giving a portrayal to rank with his finest. In Miss Susan Strasberg's poignant and entrancing Anne, Broadway is witnessing the début of an actress for whom stardom is virtually unavoidable."

The cast, the director, and the Hacketts received almost all the stage prizes of the 1955–1956 season, including the prestigious Pulitzer Prize for drama, the Tony Award, and the New York Critics' Circle Award for Best Play.

The reviews in Dutch newspapers were also favorable, although there were exceptions. Ies Spetter wrote a critical review in the former resistance paper *Vrij Nederland* with the headline "Hiding Fun on Broadway" about the "unacceptable success of Anne Frank's diary":

This whole stage performance is sacrilege, sacrilege towards the child Anne Frank, who after all wrote everything in *her* diary and sacrilege towards all those who were tortured during the occupation. Theater is theater and needs dramatic exaggeration. Therefore Anne is a bit more sexy with the use of sweaters and such than is the case for the sort of girl she was. Her father is a bit too much the thoughtful, warm, sensible, noble Jew, and resistance member, Miep, is a bit too lively and jolly, Aryan, optimistic by nature, and "we'll help you poor Jews." [...] There are things that are sacred, and Broadway should not touch them.

Of course, the adaptation of a book, or in this case a diary, is not a literal rendering of the original. But the fact that Hitler existed, as did National Socialism, that there was anti-Semitism, and that Anne was persecuted because she was Jewish—all disappeared into the background in the play. Moreover, an obvious change of roles occurred during the stage adaption. Otto Frank occupies a more prominent place in the play than Anne had given him in her diary. The play ends in November 1945, when Otto Frank and the helpers briefly recount the period after the arrest.

Although it sounds odd, the stage-Otto reports that Anne was happy in Westerbork and that he heard a short time after the war that she ended up in Bergen-Belsen. But her death remains unmentioned. Then Anne's voice is heard with the sentence that has become famous: "I still believe, in spite of everything, in the goodness of people." The play concludes with Otto's words: "She puts me to shame." Many in the audience thought, or hoped, that Anne Frank had ended her diary with this optimistic and uplifting phrase. In reality, it appears in her diary entry of July 15, 1944, two weeks before her last diary entry. Moreover, Anne writes that she believes that people are "good at heart," which is different from being generally "good."

In *Het Achterhuis*, Pfeffer, the dentist, whose name was changed to Dussel by Anne, is shown in a negative light. Anne thought he was "slow-witted," and he "went down in her estimation." In the play, his character is even more negative. Charlotte Pfeffer-Kaletta wrote acrimoniously to the Hacketts that her husband was portrayed as a psychopath in the play. Because of the Nuremberg laws, Charlotte and Pfeffer had not been able to marry in Germany and also not in the Netherlands where they had fled in 1938 because Dutch bureaucrats followed Hitler's laws even before the war. She married him posthumously in 1953. Otto Frank was helpful with this. He also helped her financially on repeated occasions; this is evident from a statement signed by her and Otto Frank in 1956 in which Otto declared that he would not ask for the money he lent her and she renounced all claims to *Het Achterhuis*, the play, and the movie. She was more or less bought off.

The most negative role in the play was that of Mr. van Pels, whose name was changed by Anne to Van Daan. He was caught stealing food the evening before the Allied invasion of Normandy, and Anne's mother shouted angrily that he had to leave. This scene occurs nowhere in Anne's diary; it's a dramatic addition by the playwrights. At first, Bloomgarden had decided that Dussel, the dentist, would steal the bread, but it became Van Daan. However, his brother lived in New York, and Otto Frank, who was closely involved in the realization of the play, feared eventual legal consequences. This exceptionally negative portrayal of Van Daan remained in the play despite his brother's protests.

Because of the New York success, interest in the play increased in Europe, and it seemed logical that this 1955 Pulitzer Prize winner would be represented at the International Theater Festival in Paris the following spring. But in 1956 there was a break with this tradition: *The Diary of Anne Frank* would not be performed in Paris. According to a Dutch daily paper (*De Telegraaf*), this happened because of pressure by the American Department of State, which didn't want to adversely influence the still fragile French-German relations by such a reminder of the war. This is why Sweden had the European premiere, followed by both West and East Germany. Remarkably, the play was performed in both countries on the same day, and a headline in a Dutch ex-resistance paper (*Trouw*) read as follows: "*The Diary of Anne Frank* conquers Germany." The reactions differed considerably, although in both countries there had been a long silence after the performance. The audience left the auditorium silently and with "feelings of shame," or they applauded longer than after any other play. "*Diary of Anne Frank* stirs people's conscience" was the almost triumphant mention in one of the Dutch papers.

The Play in the Netherlands

"[Het] Achterhuis also on the Dutch stage? A special company may have to be formed because none of our companies may be able to satisfy the conditions. But it's already in Great Britain and in German speaking countries."

These were the first lines of a newspaper article (*De Telegraaf*), but Otto Frank fortunately agreed to a performance in the Netherlands. Louis de Jong of the NIOD had written to Otto that *Toneelgroep Theater* was the obvious choice, according to the director of the Amsterdam Theater School. Moreover, the actor Bob de Vries had played "an outstanding role in the resistance, and he would therefore do everything to create as perfect an atmosphere as possible." It was done accordingly, and under the direction of Karl Guttmann, Otto Frank was played by Rob de Vries and Anne by Martine Crefcoeur, who was still in theater school. Edith Frank was played by Jenny van Maetlant. Jules Croiset played Peter van Daan, and Enny Mols-de

Leeuwe and Hans Tiemeyer his parents, while Bernhard Droog performed the role of Dussel.

The premiere was at the end of November 1956 in the De La Mar Theater in Amsterdam. "Masterful performance by *Toneelgroep Theater*" was a newspaper (*Het Parool*) headline, and the critic continued: "I have to admit that I have never before experienced such an overwhelming and massive emotion in a theater. There was no applause. The audience, among whom Queen Juliana and Prince Bernhard and the mayor d'Ailly of Amsterdam and many other prominent figures, left in silence."

There was praise everywhere for the Dutch performance, which had taken on an almost sacred significance. In the Jewish weekly (*Nieuw Israëlitisch Weekblad*), Simon van Collum said that he had honestly been quite suspicious, but that it hadn't become a "Broadway hit" and that it was a "very moving performance." He especially praised the role of Rob de Vries ("the Jewish boy . . . who was so eager to be on stage"): "It is understandable that a critic of a religious weekly wrote that it's almost profane to write about his creation and that in many of his high points he almost resembles a saint."

Even a more intellectual Jewish magazine (*Levend Joods Geloof*) sang the praises of the play and pointed out an aspect "that made the greatest impression on the non-Jews in the audience. One might call it the function of Jewish suffering in which the voice of God is heard, calling on humanity to learn the lessons and to continue until the unity of mankind is a fact."

Anne had reached a new public. The play was performed every few years by professional companies (a favorite date was May 4, the World War II memorial day in the Netherlands), and it is also often performed by amateur companies and in schools and universities. The intellectual character of the performances has lessened over the years. At the Dutch premiere of the 1985 revival, the Royal House was once again represented, this time by Princess Margriet, a sister of the queen.

The play was seen as a monument, a monument like Anne Frank herself, and the Netherlands seemed to be confirmed in its self-image as a courageous country. The play was performed in Jerusalem in 1957 on the eve of the commemoration of the 1941 February strike in Amsterdam, which was a protest against the anti-Jewish campaign of the Nazis. The mayor of Jerusalem wired his colleague in Amsterdam that the performance was a tribute "to the population of Amsterdam, whose love of freedom and compassion for the victims of hate and savage madness during the Nazi occupation formed a beacon of light during the darkness before the Netherlands regained its freedom and sovereignty."

It is striking that "compassion" was mentioned and not "resistance"—a historically correct presentation of things.

Starting in the fall of 1955, the creation of Anne Frank's image would be determined fundamentally by the stage adaptation in which her father had been very closely involved.

Even before the play was performed in the Netherlands, a committee was formed in Amsterdam to erect an Anne Frank monument, but that didn't go without a struggle. The daily paper of the Social Democratic party (*Het Vrije Volk*) protested against the committee because some of its members were Communists, and the Jewish weekly objected to the initiative itself. The weekly thought that it was unnecessary "to place the weight of all of Dutch Jewry on Anne." A memorial site had already been chosen; oddly, it wasn't the hiding place on Prinsengracht but instead the *Hollandsche Schouwburg* (Dutch Theater) on Plantage Middenlaan. During the Second World War, this theater had been the collection place of Jews who were to be deported from Amsterdam. It would now be changed into a "memorial garden" in memory of Anne Frank, although Anne herself had never been there. The plan did not come off, but a year later, the Anne Frank House was established; its purpose was to preserve the building at 263 Prinsengracht and to spread Anne's ideals. There were no Communists on the board of the Anne Frank House; instead there were Amsterdam dignitaries like Truus Wijsmuller. Before the war, she had been exceptionally active in bringing almost ten thousand Jewish children from Germany and Austria to safety. During the war, she was active in the resistance, and after the war, she represented the liberal party on the Amsterdam city council.

A few years later, the city of Amsterdam established the *Hollandsche Schouwburg* as a memorial to the persecution of Jews.

Lawsuit around the Play

Meanwhile, in the United States, the rejected Levin hadn't been idle, for he continued to believe that his own version of the play was better than the Broadway hit of the Hacketts. The great success of the play had angered him even more. He decided to make his objections public and did this rather conspicuously. On January 13, 1954, he placed an ad in the theater page of the *New York Post* in which he challenged producer Kermit Bloomgarden to perform a public test reading of Levin's adaptation. In this way, his adaptation would get a fair chance, and he was convinced that it would turn out to be the "right one." Levin was increasingly seeking publicity and was seen by more and more people as a stubborn complainer and a poor loser. The opposition that he experienced strengthened him in his idea that people were plotting against him. He found a lawyer who believed in his case and decided to take the case to court.

At the end of 1956, Meyer Levin brought charges against Otto Frank and Kermit Bloomgarden before the Supreme Court of New York. He claimed that fraud and breach of contract had been committed and that the Hacketts had made use of his material without asking and without paying. Furthermore, he wanted to be able to release his own version in Israel. According to him, this had been in the earlier contract with Otto Frank. Levin demanded a total of $200,000 in damages, and for the time being, he had the proceeds of the play attached. In a written defense all the charges were refuted, and the judge dismissed the charges of fraud and breach of contract. The judge brought the charge of plagiarism before a jury, which decided that there had indeed been plagiarism and that Levin was entitled to damages of $50,000. Of course, plagiarism was difficult to prove because the authors of both plays had used one source: the diary. Partly because of this, the judge set aside the jury's verdict and decided that the matter had to be heard again.

Levin also remained active outside the courtroom and made many efforts to influence public opinion. He gave lectures everywhere, bombarded spokesmen of the Jewish community with numerous pamphlets, and wrote many letters to the editor. In one of these, he wrote that there were two ways to destroy Jewish life. The first way was physical—the Nazis had done that. The second way was the destruction of Jewish culture: "In some countries this happens through the eradication of Jewish culture." According to him, the refusal to perform his play was an obvious example of this. Ultimately, Levin managed to get Eleanor Roosevelt on his side, and she wrote a letter to Otto Frank in which she pressured him to back Levin. Roosevelt went quite far in this by stating that in a potential lawsuit unfortunate matters would be revealed—for example, that Otto Frank had moved to Switzerland to avoid the high Dutch taxes. Later, the president's widow would distance herself from Levin, but her letter clearly shows his power of persuasion. Levin used the questionable suggestion that Otto Frank had "fled" to Switzerland to evade income taxes on other occasions.

Eventually, Levin suggested that a committee of "wise men" from the American Jewish community should try to reach a compromise. All those involved agreed, and there seemed to be a compromise. In the fall of 1959, an agreement was reached whereby Meyer Levin received $15,000 and assigned all his rights to a stage adaptation to Otto Frank. This also concerned a possible Hebrew version. Moreover, both parties would no longer discuss the play publicly, which primarily meant that Meyer Levin would henceforth have to hold his tongue.

The matter seemed settled, something that must have been very good for Levin's marriage, since at a certain point his wife was completely fed up with his actions. However, Levin didn't stop and continued to argue his case in synagogues and other Jewish institutions. In 1973, when he published a book about his involvement in the diary of Anne Frank, he chose the appropriate title *The Obsession*. In it he wrote, among other things, that the committee of "wise men"—please note, chosen by him—had been unfit and that he had become the victim of a McCarthy-style persecution. During the McCarthy hearings of the House Un-American Activities Committee, Lillian Hellmann managed to get off unscathed by informing the committee that she had long ago concluded that she wasn't a political person and therefore would not have felt comfortable in a political party. Like many others, she was blacklisted as a Communist and couldn't work in Hollywood for a long time. In Meyer Levin's eyes, Lillian Hellman was the evil genius: as a member of the American-Jewish establishment of German origin, she looked down on Jews from Eastern Europe like Levin. For Levin, it was no longer just about Anne Frank, but also about what it was like to be a Jew in America.

Levin succeeded in reaching his goal in life, the performance of his version, although for a short time. At the end of 1966, he saw a chance to have the play performed in Tel Aviv by a theater company of the Israeli army. The Israeli press gave favorable reviews and remarked that this version was more real than that of the Hacketts. Levin had wisely withheld the fact that he no longer had rights to his play, but Otto Frank's lawyers soon found out about this illegal performance. They demanded a stop, and to Levin's great displeasure, there was an end to the performances. Later, a few performances took place in the United States, but it was clear that Levin couldn't remotely equal the Goodrich-Hackett success.

Levin's most important point was that his adaptation had been rejected because it was "too Jewish." There were many religious Jewish and Zionistic elements in his adaptation, and Otto Frank cared little for any of that. Moreover, there are hardly any religious Jewish or Zionist aspects in Anne's diary. She writes briefly about Zionism early in her diary when she hadn't gone into hiding yet. One of her friends goes "to a club organized by the Zionists" (June 30, 1942), but Anne herself doesn't talk about it. According to her, Margot felt differently: "I can assure you, I'm not so set on a bourgeois life as Mother and Margot. I'd like to spend a year in Paris and London learning the languages and studying art history. Compare that with Margot, who wants to nurse newborns in Palestine" (May 8, 1944).

A telling example of Otto Frank's assimilation is the passage of November 3, 1943, in which he suggests giving Anne a copy of the New Testament for Hanukkah: "'Are you planning to give Anne a Bible for Hanukkah?' Margot asked, somewhat perturbed. 'Yes . . . Well, Maybe St. Nicholas Day would be a better occasion,' Father replied. Jesus and Hanukkah don't exactly go together." Otto Frank included this passage unchanged in *Het Achterhuis*—an example of his assimilation?

And what should we think of a passage of March 7, 1944? "Then the second half of 1943, my body became adult and my spirit underwent a very, very great change, I became acquainted with God!" The version rewritten by Anne is the following: "The second half of the year was slightly better. I became a teenager, and was treated more like a grownup." Exit God. Jaap Meijer, a Dutchman, wasn't far off the mark in his 1947 book review in which he remarked that any Jewish orientation was completely lacking in Anne.

Levin's criticism of Goodrich and Hackett's making the diary non-Jewish and of their "universalizing" was and is shared by many people, but whether his own version did justice to Anne remains a moot point. In his loathing of the adaptation, Levin emphasized the "poisonous role" of Lillian Hellman. At the time, he was probably not aware of the very significant influence of Otto Frank, especially during the early phases of the stage adaptation. Levin felt he had a moral claim on Anne Frank, whom he had "discovered" for the American market. As he wrote in *The Obsession*, "Here was the voice I had been waiting for, the voice from among themselves, the voice from the mass grave"

Nevertheless, it's a fact that the play, more than the book, has determined the image of Anne Frank for the greater public: a happy, lively girl who falls in love and sometimes has profound thoughts. Anne has become the symbol of universal human suffering rather than "the voice of six million vanished [Jewish] souls."

For some time, a special cassette has been for sale in the United States with sound effects such as the bells of the Westertoren, a barrel organ, and "drunken soldiers singing 'Lili Marlene.'" Amateur theater groups can use this cassette as background for performances.

The "New" Play

The American publication of the "new" *Diary of a Young Girl* in 1995 created renewed interest in the play. During all these years, no change had been allowed in the Goodrich and Hackett version. The many years of criticism of the non-Jewish character of the play led to the Anne Frank Foundation asking the American playwright Wendy Kesselman to adapt the play. They didn't want a new play, but instead asked that the Goodrich-Hackett version be reworked with a minimum of two-thirds of the play remaining intact. This new version had its premiere at the end of 1997.

The historical context of the play was expressed more clearly in this version, and the role of Otto was diminished in favor of Anne's role. The play doesn't begin in 1945, when Otto Frank reads the diary after his return, but at the moment that the Frank family goes into hiding. The famous closing sentence, "Despite everything I believe in the goodness of people," still appears, but not at the end—this time, the audience is informed at the end about what happened to Anne and the other people in hiding. The publicity often mentioned that the play had been made less Jewish, which supposedly happened in the fifties, but that it would be restored in this new version. For example, a Hanukkah song was now sung in Hebrew. At the time, Goodrich and Hackett had chosen the English version of the song so as not to burden the American public with something unintelligible to them. In one of the scenes, Dussel, the dentist, even prays wearing a prayer shawl. The new version reflects a "politically correct Judaism," characteristic of the United States in the nineties. But there was a slow shift to the ideas of Levin. Levin, who died in 1981, would have been pleased. He would also have been content that his struggle about Anne was central in the play *Compulsion*, by Rinne Groff, which was performed in New York early in 2011.

The New Dutch Version of 2014

Almost sixty years after the first play, a completely new version was created—*ANNE*, written by the Jewish husband-and-wife team Leon de Winter and Jessica Durlacher, both well-known Dutch writers. The starting point was the same, the diary of Anne Frank. Their predecessors of 1955 had only the English translation of *Het Achterhuis* at their disposal, but because all of Anne's writings have been published since 1986, Durlacher and De Winter had richer sources to draw on. That is clearly visible in some areas, but the approach is substantially different than in 1955. In this latest version, the real names of the people in hiding are used for the first time, not the aliases that Anne gave them.

The 1955 version stayed dutifully between 1942 and 1944, with a very brief moment of Otto Frank's return in 1945. The play *ANNE* starts shortly after the war in Paris, where Anne meets a publisher. She doesn't want to let him read her "biography" because she "can only let someone read it who . . . loves me." But she is willing to tell him what she experienced, and then she starts with her thirteenth birthday when they still lived on Merwedeplein in Amsterdam. Among other things, she received a red-plaid autograph album that she started to use as a diary. The play then follows the story as it actually happened: going into hiding, the arrival of the Van Pels family and, later, Pfeffer (the dentist), the difficulties, the bickering, moments of joy, and being fearful for their lives. What happens in the outside world, and to their friends and acquaintances? The outside world also comes very close because of the dogfights above Amsterdam and bombings of the city.

But Anne writes and writes and slowly falls in love with Peter van Pels, although her heart still goes out to her earlier love, Peter Schiff. Pfeffer still acts as a practicing Jew as in the 1997 Kesselman version, praying before he goes to bed, wearing a yarmulke, but without a prayer shawl. Hermann van Pels no longer steals while he is in hiding, but at a certain point, he and his family live off Otto Frank. In her diary, Anne writes only that their money is totally gone. The greatest change is in the role of Otto Frank, who used to dominate. He is still very important and authoritarian but is no longer the domineering "camp counselor" father of 1955. The role of Otto's wife has become more complex, and she is no longer the bad mother who is not loved by Anne. The audience experiences the raid and the deportation of those in hiding, and the play concludes with Otto Frank relating how the others died.

This version of the play has become "the diary of Anne Frank, the writer" and is in this way a worthy successor to the Goodrich-Hackett version, which was more "the diary of Otto Frank."

Anne Frank in Hollywood: The Movie

ON OCTOBER 18, 1942, ANNE writes next to a small photo in her first diary: "This is a photo of me as I would like to look all the time. Then I might have a chance of getting to Hollywood. But at present, unfortunately, I usually look quite different."

In "Delusions of Stardom," a story that Anne wrote around Christmas 1943, she goes to Hollywood as a seventeen-year-old beauty: "We flew for nearly 5 days. On the evening of the 5th day we arrived at a place not far from Hollywood." Photo shoots and advertising photos are made of Anne. After a week, she is exhausted and is "cured once and for all of all [. . .] delusions of fame."

She was crazy about movie stars and pasted lots of their pictures on the wall of her room in their hiding place. But from 1944 on, it is clear that she would prefer to be a writer or a journalist.

The Holocaust on the Big Screen

After the success of *The Diary of Anne Frank* on Broadway, nothing really stood in the way of a movie adaptation. In the fall of 1956, Twentieth Century Fox obtained the movie rights, and now Hollywood could show that it was more than a fun factory. The movie, which was finished in 1959, is interesting for several reasons. First, it is one of the earliest Hollywood productions in which the Holocaust, though playing a principal role, is deliberately not shown.

According to Annette Insdorf, an American film historian, the movie was the first "Hollywood version of the Holocaust" Even though *The Diary of Anne Frank* was no box office success, it did make the diary better known.

46

The movie is also one of the few films where the book is better known than the movie. The issue "trivializing" the Holocaust was touched on in 1959, but this didn't actually emerge until later. Subsequently, the movie was denounced as an example of trivializing and Americanizing the Holocaust.

A "real" Oscar-winning Hollywood director, George Stevens, was chosen and took on the production as well. He had been making movies since the twenties and had built up a solid reputation, but what seemed more important for this movie was that Stevens had war experience as a filmmaker. During the Second World War, he had crossed Europe in the wake of American troops as the head of an Army Signal Corps film unit. He filmed the liberation of Denmark and was among the first Americans to visit Hitler's house in Berchtesgaden. His images of the survivors of the Dachau concentration camp were seen all over the world. In addition to the official thirty-five-millimeter black-and-white shots, he was one of the very few filmmakers who also made sixteen-millimeter color shots. According to his son, George Stevens Jr., the war had not changed his father, but rather, had given his work more depth. That was expressed in *A Place in the Sun*, which received no less than six Oscars in 1951, including one for himself as director. In 1956 he also received an Oscar for *Giant*.

Goodrich and Hackett would write the screenplay, and it was already decided that it would differ very little from their stage adaptation. Where play and movie do differ is in the important role played by Mouschi, Peter's cat. Mouschi contributed greatly to the tension during a break-in and search of the front part of the building by two German soldiers.

Stevens started his preparations in 1957, although the conflict around Meyer Levin had not yet been resolved. At one point, Levin offered to drop all his charges if his daughter Dominique was chosen to play the role of Anne. That was not pursued. Stevens had Otto Frank show him around the building on Prinsengracht. He also took several trips to Dachau, where he had been ten years earlier.

Who Will Play Anne?

In the Netherlands, there was some excitement when it turned out that an American film crew was going to shoot in Amsterdam and that a Dutch girl might possibly get the principal part. It would have been natural for Susan Strasberg, who had played Anne very successfully on Broadway, to take on the role. But according to Shelley Winters, who was going to play Mrs. Van Daan in the movie, Susan was involved in her first love affair, with no less than Richard Burton: "The thought of having to leave Burton for a day was more than she wanted to contemplate." But Stevens really wanted a new face for the movie-Anne, and that meant he preferred an unknown amateur to a well-known actress. In Stevens's words: "The girl who will give shape to Anne must be a sweet, simple girl, a child that every man and every woman would want to care for by placing a protective arm around her."

There were indeed high expectations when Stevens's talent scout, Owen McLean, came to Amsterdam at the end of 1957 to test seventy Dutch girls to see whether they were suitable for the role. He had already received 2,500 letters from prospective Annes, the majority from the Netherlands. Meanwhile, screen tests were also conducted in other countries, and there was even a rumor that a non-Jewish German girl had a good chance. An outraged newspaper comment read as follows: "Will Fox dare to provoke the feelings of such an important part of its public in this way?" The rather new Anne Frank House threatened to cancel all cooperation with the movie if that happened.

Accompanied with much fanfare, a Dutch candidate seemed to have a good chance: fifteen-year-old Marianna Sarstädt, a dancer with the Amsterdam Scapino Ballet and half-Jewish, according to some papers. Other names considered for the role of Anne Frank were Audrey Hepburn and Romy Schneider. The first one might be possible; after all, she had experienced the battle for Arnhem as a teenager. In 1984 her biographer Charles Higham wrote: "According to Audrey, who had resisted the Nazis day and night from the very beginning [. . .] it was the courage as personified by her unforgettable fellow countrywoman Anne Frank." Ten years after this biography, Hepburn, the former "resistance fighter," managed to remember much more about the prospective movie role. She remembered that Otto Frank had even visited her to convince her, but Audrey claimed that she identified so much with Anne that she couldn't do it.

And Romy Schneider? The newspaper *Het Vrije Volk* wrote: "Because Romy Schneider's purely Germanic appearance shows so little resemblance to the Jewish girl, Anne, it seems possible that her managers are spreading these reports in order to fix Americans' attention on the young German woman who clearly hopes to continue her career in Hollywood." At any rate, her movies had already been very successful in Europe.

It was quite a blow in the Netherlands when it became known that nineteen-year-old Millie Perkins, a model, would play Anne Frank. Stevens commented: "In many respects she personifies the sweet, early maturing Anne, and in addition she possesses the natural talent to perform Anne Frank true to form and in detail." In the Netherlands, there was great bitterness about these "crude American advertising methods," and the paper *Het Vrije Volk* judged harshly: "This messing around with Anne Frank's memory shows frightfully clearly how little understanding the makers of the movie actually have of the meaning that the figure of Anne Frank has in Europe and in the Netherlands in particular. Let's hope that the movie itself will at least have some good qualities."

The fact that Anne would be played by a cover girl led to negative remarks. Only one paper (*Algemeen Handelsblad*) was broad-minded in its remark that there were cover girls in the best families and there was no reason for people to look down their noses in narrow-minded bourgeois arrogance: "It's possible to be a decent person even with a captivating pretty face [. . .] especially when you're eighteen."

Otto Frank had no objection to Millie. On the contrary—according to him, she was a "sweet and fine girl" who was "sensitive and unspoiled." But that wasn't all: "Millie moves her hands exactly as Anne did."

Otto and Edith Frank and Mr. Van Daan would be played by the three who had the same roles on Broadway: Joseph Schildkraut, Gusti Huber, and Lou Jacobi. Diane Baker played Margot Frank, her first movie role. Richard Beymer played Peter van Daan; a few years later, he would play Nathalie Wood's adversary in *West Side Story*. His mother was played by Shelley Winters, who had already appeared in many movies, among others *A Place in the Sun* by Stevens. For his role as the unpleasant dentist, Dussel, Ed Wyn would receive an Oscar nomination as Best Supporting Actor.

The Cold War also played a role in the choice of actors. In the United States, the Red Scare caused the motion-picture industry to come under fire from the House Un-American Activities Committee, which looked for Communist influence in Hollywood. At the end of the 1940s, ten filmmakers, the so-called Hollywood Ten, were fined and sentenced to prison because they refused to disclose their political affiliations or blacklist their colleagues. In addition, they themselves were blacklisted, preventing them from working in the motion-picture industry. Six of the Hollywood Ten were Jews—disproportionately many when considering the number of Jews

in the United States, but there were also many Jewish motion-picture industry bosses. Therefore, movies that were "too Jewish" had to be avoided, and
that was also true for the actors, who could be Jewish but could not express
it. They had to stay away from "Jewish stereotypes." That was a difficult di-
lemma in *The Diary of Anne Frank*, but it's striking that Millie Perkins, the
movie-Anne, looks ten times more like Audrey Hepburn than like the Jewish Anne Frank. Anne as an American teenager was actually the intention
of the movie company and of Stevens, who remarked in his diary that the
movie had been a love story from the beginning. It was also assumed that
American Jews did not feel like being shadowed by European war horrors,
and certainly not during an evening out.

While some people in Amsterdam launched a campaign to prevent the
dilapidated building at 263 Prinsengracht and the Annex from being torn
down, a copy of the Annex was being built in Beverly Hills. That was where
the cast worked to create *The Diary of Anne Frank* for almost half a year.
The paper *Algemeen Dagblad* devoted an entire page to the visit of its American correspondent to the movie set. Everything had to be as authentic as
possible, and at Stevens's request, a former Dutch resistance fighter, Tonny
van Renterghem (1919–2009), monitored the set: "I'm proud of the fact that
there are no windmills and no wooden shoes in this movie! I told them that
I'd leave if they can't stick to that. Not even a Dutch gin bottle, which dates
from after the war. In that respect Stevens is totally on my side. It's unbeliev-
able the great lengths to which he goes in order to keep things exactly in the
atmosphere of Holland during the war."

A few months later, the same newspaper reported that Tonny had to
stand behind the actors in a Nazi SS uniform, so that they would act with
"shivers down their spine." According to a Dutch film critic who also visited
the set, everything was being shot in an almost solemn mood, and another
visitor remarked that she had imagined a movie shoot to be much noisier.
Stevens's reaction to that comment was: "The subject is much too delicate
for that."

In the second part of her autobiography, *The Middle of My Century*, Shelley Winters wrote a lot about the movie shoots. After all, she received her
one and only Oscar as Best Supporting Actress for her role as Mrs. van Daan.
Stevens first let the actors view the films that he had made in Birkenau, and
Shelley Winters mentions that she watched over Millie: "Millie was very

worried that she knew so little about Jewish traditions or history, so I rather took her under my wing and tried to help her as much as possible. I gave her books to read, and talked to her about what the religious background of Anne Frank must have been."

She reported proudly that Stevens ordered her to gain weight so she would look older and more like the real Mrs. van Pels, and this important news also got into the Dutch papers. Then there was the real Otto Frank:

One day about four months into the shooting, George Stevens announced to us that we were having lunch with Mr. Otto Frank, the real Anne's father. He had never seen a production of the play; it would have been too difficult a thing to do. In fact, it was rather courageous of him to come and watch some of the filming this afternoon.

We all had lunch with him in our costumes, shabby, smelly wartime Dutch clothes. He looked around the table at all the actors who were portraying his friends and family. He was trembling, and he had tears in his eyes.

Afterward, when Otto predicted that Shelley would win an Oscar, he couldn't do anything wrong in her eyes. She promised him on the spot that she would donate the Oscar to the Anne Frank House in Amsterdam, and that's what she did seventeen years later. Otto Frank, in his nineties at the time, was present on that occasion. After a few years, the Oscar was placed behind glass because young visitors frequently imitated an acceptance speech while holding the Oscar.

It was as difficult for Stevens as it had been for the producers of the play to make those in hiding visible in a rather small space. The president of the movie company insisted that CinemaScope or wide screen had to be used, a format that was meant to compete with television. However, Stevens feared that this wide screen would interfere with the intimacy and claustrophobia of the movie. Nevertheless, he had to shoot with this broad and technically not yet perfected format in which closeups were distorted. Shelley Winters also mentioned the CinemaScope problems: "It seems CinemaScope was going to be Hollywood's answer to television, which in 1958 they were still pretending would go away. If people were watching pictures on a small little box, they were going to entice them away from that free little box with a huge horizontal screen. While CinemaScope was great for photographing Niagara Falls or Westerns or any outdoor spectacle, it was not very useful when photographing actors' thoughts and feelings."

A solution to creating intimacy was found by emphasizing vertical beams like walls, which would work as extra frames, instead of horizontal beams like ceiling rafters. A part of the scenery was placed on springs so that the Annex could actually shake during the bombing scene. Optimal use of sound was made in this scene, and it was used a lot (among other things, marching Germans, marching music, gunshots, and of course, the bells of the Westertoren) to represent the outside world.

Hollywood Comes to Amsterdam

While Stevens was shooting in Hollywood, his son was taking care of the outdoor scenes on location. This was naturally of great interest in the Netherlands. After all, Hollywood didn't often come to Amsterdam, and the delivery of thousands of kilos of artificial snow for making winter shots in the summer really appealed to people's imaginations. However, the plan to uproot a large number of trees and replace them first by artificial trees and, after the shooting, by real trees was not carried out. That would have been too expensive, and therefore they settled for only one leafless tree, which seemed to satisfy the Dutch press.

During that time, the musicians of the American Federation of Musicians were on strike against the movie bosses, and the Dutch Musicians Union, later followed by the Catholic Union, had called on its members not to act as strike breakers. A German military band was supposed to play during the shoots, and the director had called up Dutch musicians for this. But these musicians didn't really have to play, since the sound would be mixed later. The Amsterdam Police Band would have been glad to play, but not in German uniforms. According to a newspaper (*Het Vrije Volk*): "Police nixes German costumes." A band, Harmonie Tuindorp Oostzaan, also withdrew its earlier commitment when the members heard of the boycott. In the end, conservatory students and musicians recruited in bars in Amsterdam performed, but there was a complaint that they didn't walk stiffly enough to pass for marching German soldiers.

There was also a call for Jewish extras, preferably in family groups and in the right kind of clothing. It is rather unclear whether the call-up yielded the desired result, but in the movie there is a roundup on Staalstraat in Amsterdam. Thanks to the Ministry of Defense, Stevens obtained a helicopter, which was used during the shooting of the roundup scene.

A Successful Movie?

In one of the first versions of the movie, Anne was in a concentration camp. That scene was eliminated after a preview because the audience reacted in disbelief to such a realistic depiction. Anne Frank was and remained the girl who wrote a diary, not the girl who had experienced the horrors of a camp.

In the Netherlands, people were under the impression that the world premiere would take place in Amsterdam. The City and Rialto movie theaters were mentioned as likely candidates for this honor, but the world premiere was, of course, held in the United States. Supporters of the civil rights movement were present; after all, Anne Frank didn't exclusively symbolize the persecution of Jews there.

This had obviously not been noticed by the *Nieuw Israëlitisch Weekblad* (Dutch Jewish Weekly), which, under the heading "Good screen version of Anne Frank," reported: "The audience, naturally consisting primarily of Jews, had dressed up for the evening; ladies in their fur coats and gentlemen, some in tuxedos, conversed in a most cheerful manner, as if they were going to an evening of great entertainment. Fortunately my expectations were not met this time. [...] In conclusion it should be said that this movie is certainly one of the few that are worth seeing."

The prominent critic A. J. P. van Domburg seemed moderately satisfied in the May issue of *Filmforum* as he declared that Americans naturally viewed the movie differently than the Dutch. But he did think that Stevens had treated "the delicate material with the necessary respect."

Despite eight Oscar nominations, three of which were actually awarded, the movie wasn't very successful in America. The movie did lead to a new interest in the book, and according to Otto, it had a great influence on "publishing the diary in other countries."

According to a Dutch weekly (*Haagsche Post*), the author Remco Campert translated the subtitles into Dutch. In April 1959, the European premiere took place in the Netherlands, and the atmosphere was just as solemn as at the first performance of the play two and a half years earlier. Queen Juliana and Crown Princess Beatrix were present, and most of the audience had complied with the request to wear dark clothing. At the end of the performance, the audience stood to listen to the Dutch national anthem. Jaap van der Merwe, who reviewed the movie for *Het Vrije Volk*, was of the opinion that it had become the diary of Otto Frank and Anne was merely one of the principal characters.

International movie magazines were not very charitable, and that was chiefly because the relationship between Anne and Peter was so prominent. Nevertheless, the German magazine *Filmkritik* found the movie "acceptable" but objected to the fact that the movie stuck too closely to the play and that CinemaScope didn't work well during the dialogues. Moreover, "the sexual awakening of a very impressionable girl is reduced to teenage love." The *Monthly Filmbulletin* wasn't much more favorable: "*The Diary of Anne Frank* shows Hollywood at its most honourable and its least imaginative . . . , reduced to the level of any boy-meets-girl romance."

Sight and Sound International Film Quarterly also connected the movie inextricably to Hollywood: "But style is of little use when the subject is beyond its creator's imaginative range: consequently *The Diary of Anne Frank* fell a victim to Hollywood's craze for overblown portentousness as well as to its general miscasting. In a way, the sad failure of this film seems to sum up a whole epoch of Hollywood thinking."

To everyone's surprise, *The Diary of Anne Frank* was the only American movie shown at the second International Film Festival in Moscow in 1962. The United States boycotted this film festival because it and the Soviet Union were involved in a bitter dispute about cinema rights of each other's movies. The Russians showed Stevens's movie, but it could not compete for prizes. Shelley Winters, who was present at the festival, wondered about this: "I tried to find out why *Anne Frank* was entered OUT of competition. After many vodka toasts the only thing I understood was that the plight of Anne Frank and her family was not politically correct according to the Soviet party line."

In other words, the persecuted Jews shouldn't have gone into hiding defenselessly but should have fought against fascism. Yet there is a scene in the movie in which the residents want to defend themselves, and the viewer sees Otto Frank holding an axe, threatening. However, this was because of a burglar and not because of the Germans.

Millie Perkins, the female lead, came for a visit to the Netherlands at the end of 1959, exhausted from a long publicity tour. One of the newspapers reported "unpleasant hawking of the young actress." It seemed as if the matters around the movie were more important than the movie itself. In the June issue of *Filmforum*, under the heading "Millianne," Van Domburg complained about Millie being dragged around through Amsterdam and other cities: "Bad taste has broken through again and there is going to be hell to pay. Not only the entrepreneurs but also the tabloids are cashing in on the sensitivities, and they're hardly the only ones."

In addition, Van Domburg quotes the newsmagazine *De Tijd*, which is also quite critical:

One would think that it's enough. But the advertising business wants to have their cake and eat it too. [...] We feel that this spectacle is becoming disgusting. One can't blame the businessmen in America for not sensing these matters. After all, they didn't experience the occupation. But there is an administration of the Anne Frank House, which could have prevented these spectacles.

We would still like to add something to this opinion. It seems to us that it isn't the American lack of understanding of the occupation but simple greed that barely knows limits and is not afraid of taking advantage of any opportunity to get what they want.

Her visit and even the presentation of a new variety of red Millie Perkins roses would not help Millie, as her fame soon evaporated. Two years later, she had a small role in Elvis Presley's third movie, *Wild in the Country*. She herself spoke, and not without justification, of an "Anne Frank hangover." And although Anne Frank has in the meantime been played by thousands of girls throughout the whole world, for many people Millie Perkins remained *the* Anne Frank; for a considerable time, her photo adorned the cover of the American edition of Anne's diary. In 1991 she was again in the Netherlands for a short time, but this time on glossy photos. The photo archives of Spaarnestad had organized a small photo exhibition around Millie, and a beautiful catalog was made for the occasion.

It's strange that a movie based on a very successful play was less popular than expected. We may have to look for the explanation in the American sociopolitical situation at the time; this was personified in a beautiful photo, taken during the New York movie premiere, of Shelley Winters as well as Martin Luther King Jr., Harry Belafonte, and both their wives. For millions of Americans, who wanted nothing to do with black civil rights, this photo must have been a sign to stay away: a Jewish actress with left-wing ideas, who supported the civil rights movement of which King was the undisputed leader. Many American Jews had—as lawyer, lobbyist, or activist—supported the black struggle for civil rights.

Anne's Diary under Attack

WHEN THE DIARY OF ANNE Frank was not yet world famous, no one doubted its authenticity or Anne's short existence. After the publication of *Das Tagebuch* in Germany in 1959, there certainly were questions about her too-mature language. The translator was usually blamed, and deservedly.

Two years after the 1955 premiere of the play in the United States, the first attack on the authenticity of Anne's diary was launched. The Danish anti-Semitic literary critic Harald Nielsen published the article "Jewish Psyche—A Study about Anne Frank and Meyer Levin" in the Swedish National Socialist paper *Fria Ord*. He questioned the authenticity of the diary and stated that Meyer Levin was its actual author. During the next half century, that would be the most important argument of the deniers of the diary's authenticity. Hadn't a judge in New York ordered Otto Frank to pay Meyer Levin for his work? The fact that the lawsuit was about the play and *Het Achterhuis* had been published in 1947, well before Levin and Otto Frank had met, was disregarded. In various media, primarily those of the extreme right, the deniers constantly referred to each other as "proof" that the denial was true. Harald Nielsen, who had earlier written anti-Semitic articles, also pointed out that Anne and Peter were not Jewish names, in contrast to the name Meyer Levin.

Almost half a year later, a Norwegian magazine (*Folge og Land*), the mouthpiece of the former Viking SS division, took up the baton. Referring to the court case in New York, the article determined that the diary was most likely a forgery. A part of that article appeared in translation in *Reichsruf Wochenzeitung für das nationale Deutschland*, a weekly paper of the extreme right *Deutsche Reichspartei*, established in 1950.

These publications were read almost exclusively by their own rank and file, and no action was taken against them by Otto Frank or any of the publishers. That changed in 1958 with Lothar Stielau, an English teacher at the *Oberschule zum Dom* in Lübeck. Stielau, fifty years old at the time, had been a member of the Nazi Party (NSDAP) and the storm troopers (SA), a member of the *Deutsche Reichspartei* after the war, and district chairman of its Lübeck group.

Stielau had written a review of the performance of the play *The Adventures of Tom Sawyer* in the school's alumni magazine on October 10, 1958. Halfway through his essay, he wrote: "The forged diaries of Eva Braun, of the Queen of England, and the hardly more authentic one of Anne Frank may have earned several millions for the profiteers from Germany's defeat, but they have also raised our own hackles quite a bit."

Until then, nothing had happened regarding the neo-Nazi activities in Norway, Sweden, and Austria, but this time legal action was initiated. The *Zentralrat der Juden in Deutschland* had alerted Fischer publishing to the piece, and Fischer discussed it with Otto Frank. Stielau would get into trouble on two fronts because of his statements.

First, his employer, the Ministry of Culture of the state of Schleswig-Holstein, started an investigation; then, after a criminal complaint was lodged by Otto Frank and two publishers, the Ministry of Justice took action.

The Ministry of Culture investigated whether Stielau had breached his professional obligation of political neutrality, and Stielau had to explain what he meant. Stielau dressed the story up nicely by saying that he didn't doubt that Anne had kept a diary, but he was also of the opinion that no published diary resembled the original version. He felt that he could have expressed it better, but he thought he was a good educator. Of course, Stielau had supporters, among them his political superior, the chairman of the *Deutsche Reichspartei* in Schleswig-Holstein, Heinrich Buddeberg, a farmer who had been in prison for two years after the war because of Nazi activities. He defended Stielau in the *Lübecker Nachrichten* by writing that Stielau was a political victim of the Social Democrats, and he brought up Meyer Levin again. Buddeberg would later be charged with slander and defamation. Stielau was suspended temporarily because he was suspected of having neglected his duties and was unworthy of the esteem and trust that were part of the teaching profession. Moreover, his political attitude was not consistent with the educational mission of the school; all in all, that was sufficient reason for a temporary suspension.

The public prosecutor's office of Schleswig-Holstein reacted quickly. There was an answer two days after a criminal complaint (which included libel, slander, insult, defamation of the memory of a dead person, and anti-Semitic utterances) was lodged on behalf of Otto Frank and the two publishing houses. Moreover, the federal minister of justice in Bonn asked his colleague in Schleswig-Holstein to keep him informed. It was clear that the young German Federation was sensitive about its Nazi past. The public prosecutor in Lübeck expressed it as follows: "Given the delicate nature of the attitude of foreign countries towards Germany and her people due to their National Socialist past, a judicial inquiry is the only way of arriving at a satisfactory conclusion."

In his memorandum, the public prosecutor also referred to an article in *Der Spiegel* in which Cauvern was quoted: "At the beginning I made a good many changes."

An examining magistrate was appointed who questioned a number of those involved. During his second examination, Stielau asserted that his remarks didn't pertain to the diary but to the stage adaptation, a striking turn, since he hadn't said that earlier. Of course, Otto Frank was examined, as were Bep Voskuijl and Miep and Jan Gies. But their statements were not sufficient to determine the authenticity, and the examining magistrate looked for experts who would be able to do that. Annemarie Hübner of the University of Hamburg was asked to write an expert assessment of the diary. Schütz, the translator, had used typescript 2 of the diary for the translation instead of *Het Achterhuis*, which would have been the more obvious choice. Therefore, Hübner compared typescript 2 with the German translation to see whether the German could be considered a "true and faithful" translation of the original, and she described it as follows: "The translation must be considered to correspond [to the original] and on the whole to be factually correct. There are mistakes in translation and these are to be deprecated, but most of them can be considered minor faults which are immaterial to an understanding of the total context."

Her conclusion was that the German translation must be considered "true to its sources and ideas." This was a rather sloppy conclusion because the German translation had a lot of errors, certainly about things that were left out to avoid offending the German public.

Hübner's expertise was found to be insufficient, since Minna Becker, a graphologist from Hamburg, was asked to determine whether all the diary entries, a letter, and two postcards had been written by Anne. Together with an assistant, Becker traveled to Basel to investigate the handwriting, and in a report of over 130 pages, it was determined that everything they had seen was written by Anne. That didn't square with the facts, because a letter from Otto Frank and a postcard from Jacqueline van Maarsen (Jacque) that they had also seen were, of course, not written by Anne. The same was true for a number of corrections in the original diary entries, corrections that were made after the war and most likely added by Otto Frank. At the request of the court, Becker and her assistant had also compared the different diaries and concluded that the loose sheets were written after diary 1, 2, and 3.

The magistrate wasn't satisfied and asked the opinion of another expert, this time the well-known publicist Friedrich Sieburg. The only interesting point in his report was his statement that it would be odd to forge a diary of a completely unknown person.

Stielau's lawyers, Noack and Noack from Kiel, made no effort to read the reports, but at any rate they objected to Hübner's report; they felt that she couldn't be a real expert because of her academic status. In their eyes, her report was therefore "worthless." They did, however, make use of it because it stated that there were differences between the original and the German translation. The lawyers declared: "A document must be authentic word for word, or else it is not a document." But they went much further in their defense of Stielau, whereby they concentrated on the play. Stielau had not seen the play and hadn't even wanted to see it because, according to him, the American authors Goodrich and Hackett had Communist sympathies well before the war. And Stielau—such a righteous person—had been shocked by the fact that adaptations not faithful to the text had been used to make money and the cover of the American Doubleday edition had a photo not of Anne herself but of the stage-Anne.

The file became increasingly voluminous, and everything was repeated once more in the magistrate's extensive indictment. For the sake of convenience, the Stielau and Buddeberg cases were joined. They were charged with libel for denying the authenticity of Anne's diary, and with defamation for using the term "profiteers from German defeat." After another written defense from the lawyers, the Third Criminal Division of the Lübeck regional court concluded that the case of the two suspects could now finally be heard.

It didn't get that far, for in October 1961, three years after Stielau had published his article, the case was dismissed. The lawyers of both parties agreed to a settlement whereby Stielau and Buddeberg acknowledged that the diary was not a forgery and they regretted their statements to that effect. The expression of "profiteers from Germany's defeat" was also withdrawn with expressions of regret. Otto Frank and the publishers acknowledged in writing that no anti-Semitic tendencies had been noticed on the part of the defendants. In addition, Stielau would contribute 1,000 Deutsche Mark (DM) (an equivalent of $3,000 now) to the legal costs, a tenth of the total.

This unsatisfactory outcome occurred because the president of the regional court feared that if the defendants received a very light sentence, the press would again say that the court had been too lenient in its treatment of neo-Nazis. Otto Frank, who was persuaded that the authenticity of the diary had now been established, had agreed with the settlement. Later, he said he regretted the settlement because the debate about the authenticity continued. The judge, who thought he'd stayed out of range, would read the following headline in the West German newspaper *Bild* the next day: "High school teacher libels Anne Frank [. . .] but judge lets him off."

The first case around the authenticity of Anne Frank's diaries was over, but the attacks continued, and more lawsuits would follow. The diary deniers referred continually to earlier like-minded articles, but sometimes something original appeared. In October 1957, RIOD director, Louis de Jong, had written an article about Anne Frank in *Reader's Digest*. This magazine was being published in Dutch for the first time, and an article about Anne Frank seemed appropriate. The general editors judged this article to be good enough for publication in other foreign-language versions of the magazine, and in this way, the diary deniers became aware of Louis de Jong. In January 1959, an editor of the Viennese *Europa Korrespondenz* published the article *"Der Anne Frank-Skandal. Ein Beitrag zur Wahrheit"* (The Anne Frank scandal. A Contribution to the truth) in which he wrote: "The father came to Amsterdam after the war, learned about the alleged diary, did not want to publish it, but was practically forced to do so by his friends. The

Dutch journalist Louis de Jong, now director of the Netherlands Institute for War Documentation, was crucially involved in the diary, and from the publications it is clear that De Jong is the author of the book."

It was a novel thought, but De Jong had not been involved at all with the creation of *Het Achterhuis*.

Anglo-Saxon Diary Deniers

The diary deniers in the United States continued the attacks. The formerly esteemed monthly magazine *American Mercury*, which had become increasingly racist and anti-Semitic in the fifties, made itself heard loud and clear. In the summer issue of 1967, Teressa Hendry published an article with the title "Was Anne Frank's Diary a Hoax?" The answer was obvious:

> History has many examples of myths that live a longer and richer life than the truth, and may become more effective than the truth. The Western World has for some years been aware of a Jewish girl through the medium of what purports to be her personally written story, "Anne Frank's Diary." Any informed literary inspection of this book would have shown it to have been impossible as the work of a teenager.
>
> A noteworthy decision of the New York Supreme Court confirms this point of view, in that the well known [*sic*] American Jewish writer, Meyer Levin, has been awarded $50,000 to be paid him by the father of Anne Frank as an honorarium for Levin's work on the "Anne Frank Diary."
>
> Mr. Frank, in Switzerland, has promised to pay to his race-kin, Meyer Levin, not less than $50,000 because he had used the dialogue of Author Levin just as it was and "implanted" it in the diary as being his daughter's intellectual work.

Seven years later, this story was used again in *Did Six Million Really Die? The Truth at Last* by Richard Harwood, a pseudonym of Richard Verrall, who was part of the extreme right British National Front. This was the first time the diary denial was used in the broader denial of the Holocaust. The implicit thought was that if Anne Frank could be unmasked, then this would do the same for the myth of the Holocaust. This thirty-six-page pamphlet appeared in many languages and became a real bestseller among Holocaust deniers. Harwood himself had little to say about Anne's diary: "Here, then, is just one more fraud in a whole series of frauds in support of the 'Holocaust' legend and the saga of the Six Million."

In 1974, a year later, an American, A. R. Butz, wrote *The Hoax of the Twentieth Century*, using the same publisher as Harwood. It was primarily a demographic study in which the author denied the Final Solution. The diary played a subsidiary role: "I will only remark that I have looked it over and don't believe it."

A year later, the extreme right-wing British historian, David Irving, denied in the introduction of his book, *Hitler und Seine Feldherrn* (Hitler and his generals), that Anne had written a diary. For this allegation, he referred to the Levin lawsuit. Otto Frank didn't stand for this and protested successfully to the publishers; excuses followed, and Anne would no longer be mentioned in reprints. During the following decades, David Irving was regularly in the news; as one of the few academics who denied the Holocaust, he was often invited to speak in circles of the extreme right. He also landed regularly in court, and after a sensational trial, he was condemned in a London court as an anti-Semite and a racist Holocaust denier. He was declared persona non grata in Germany, Austria, and Canada because of his public Holocaust denials. At the beginning of the twenty-first century, he caused a lot of controversy. He brought charges against the American historian Deborah Lipstadt because she had called him a "Holocaust denier." After a lengthy trial, Lipstadt was acquitted of all charges, and Irving was labeled a fraudulent scholar and an inveterate Holocaust denier.

The first book of any size to be devoted exclusively to the so-called unmasking of the diary appeared in 1978. *Anne Frank Diary—A Hoax?* was written by Ditlieb Felderer from Sweden, whose own publishing house, Bible Researcher, also published books like *Zionism: The Hidden Tyranny*. This time, Felderer conceded that Meyer Levin could not be the author of Anne's diary, but he does write about Anne as a "drug addict at tender age," "teenage sex," and "the first child porno."

It is probably no accident that in the year the successful TV miniseries *Holocaust* was shown in the United States, the Institute for Historical Review was established in Torrance, California. This Institute acted as an umbrella organization for like-minded people, who pursued "revisionist" history, primarily about the Second World War. Nazi Germany was described in exclusively positive terms, and the war crimes of the Nazis were trivialized time after time. The persecution of the Jews and the existence of the gas chambers were repeatedly denied. The Institute acted as a mail-order bookseller of revisionist and blatantly Nazi literature.

Starting in 1979, the Institute organized an annual revisionist conference where European revisionists were also very welcome. The quarterly

Journal of Historical Review primarily published the lectures of these conferences. The purpose of these activities was to try to bring anti-Semitism and neo-Nazism out into the open in a scholarly way. The old adage, "the more footnotes, the more scholarly," was practiced frequently. Juggling with numbers is one of their specialties; if you compare serious studies about the Holocaust, there will always be differing numbers with regard to the number of Jewish victims, and the revisionists happily make use of those. They keep "proving" that not that many Jews were murdered—just like innocent German civilians, they supposedly died because of Allied air raids. Moreover, according to them, many Jews immigrated to the United States and changed their names once there. In the corridors of these conferences, it was also noted that too many Jews had survived the war and still controlled the media and the banking world.

In the United States, where freedom of speech is established in the First Amendment, the revisionists have little to fear of judicial intervention. During the eighties, this led to vehement discussions at American universities. Revisionists would buy a page in a student or university publication to spread Holocaust denial among the student population. Stopping the deniers would be contrary to the First Amendment, but entering into a discussion on the First Amendment gave them the appearance of scholarly credibility.

A French Holocaust and Diary Denier: Faurisson

Holocaust denial and diary denial also became more scholarly in Europe, and Robert Faurisson, a senior lecturer at the University of Lyons, took the lead. Faurisson specialized in linguistic analysis and was called in as a specialist by Heinz Roth's lawyers. In 1975, Roth, a German architect, whose own publishing house issued numerous neo-Nazi pamphlets, began to distribute pamphlets with titles like *Anne Frank's Tagebuch—eine Falschung* (Anne Frank's diary—a forgery) and *Anne Frank's Tagebuch—Der Grosse Schwindel* (Anne Frank's diary—the big fraud). He still believed the Meyer Levin story, but the Frankfurt regional court clearly didn't believe it and decided in mid-1978 that Heinz Roth would incur a maximum fine of 500,000 DM or a maximum prison sentence of six months if he stated in public that the diary was a forgery and that Otto Frank had written it together with Meyer Levin.

In contrast to previous deniers of the diary's authenticity, Faurisson had at least done research: He had examined the French translation of *Het*

Achterhuis, compared the Dutch edition with the German, spoken to Otto Frank in Basel, and studied the hiding situation and arrest in August 1944. The fact that he didn't know Dutch didn't bother him in his research. He used all this knowledge to write a report for the court in which he sought to prove that hiding in the Annex would have been impossible and, for that reason, Anne Frank could not have written a diary. This report, written in German, was originally meant for the Frankfurt regional court and would later be published in French as *Le Journal d'Anne Frank est-il authentique?* A Dutch translation was published in Belgium in 1985 with the title *Het Dagboek van Anne Frank—een vervalsing* (Anne Frank's diary—a forgery), this time without a question mark.

It goes without saying that life in hiding carried great risks, and many thousands of those in hiding fell into the hands of the Germans. It is clear from Anne's diary that for the residents of the Annex there were many dangers—for example, by making too much noise, they would be heard by others. However, in his research, Faurisson did not examine closely what hiding actually meant in practice. And in this context, he neglected the fact that the Frank family and the others hiding with them were ultimately arrested.

A characteristic example of Faurisson's way of working is the way in which he examined the problem of noise:

> Let us take the case of noise. The people in hiding, we are told, are not allowed to make the slightest noise, to the extent that if they cough they are made quickly to take some codeine. The "enemies might hear them. The walls are so "thin." (March 25, 1943). The "enemies" are very numerous: Lewin, "who knows the building well" (October 1, 1942), the men in the warehouse, the clients, the tradesmen, the postman, the cleaning woman, Slagter the night watchman, the "sanitary department," the bookkeeper, the police flushing people out of their homes, neighbors near and far, the owner of the building, etc. It is therefore improbable, even inconceivable, that Mrs. van Daan should have been in the habit of using the vacuum cleaner daily at 12:30 (August 5, 1943). Vacuum cleaners at that time were exceptionally noisy. I must ask: "Is this credible?"

Three examples will suffice to show Faurisson's method. A comparison with the diary shows that, to prove his point, Faurisson describes only part of the situations. Mrs. van Pels's vacuuming habit is mentioned by Anne on that date, but the previous sentence reveals: "The warehousemen have gone home now." On December 6, 1943, Anne writes about "resounding laughter," but Faurisson doesn't mention that Anne is writing about a Sunday evening (December 5). On November 9, 1942, Anne notes (as does Faurisson) that a sack of brown beans had burst open and "the noise was enough to wake the dead." Faurisson neglects to quote the next sentence: "Thank God there were no strangers in the house." Every time Faurisson observes that the residents were making a lot of noise, it turns out that there were no strangers nearby.

Another characteristic point illustrates Faurisson's method even better. In his story of the arrest, he mentions a witness "who, I believe, is well informed and of good faith and at the same time has a good memory. [. . .] I have promised to keep his name secret. [. . .] The name and address of this witness [. . .] have been noted in a sealed envelope." A photo of this sealed envelope is printed as an appendix to Faurisson's "investigation," albeit only in the French version of 1980; the publisher of the Dutch version wisely left out this piece of evidence.

In general, Faurisson didn't report much that was new, but his "scholarly" method and function at a French university made the requisite impression on the revisionist audience and made him better known outside that circle. Time and again, he honored the revisionist conferences in California with a visit. Faurisson was attacked by many, including his own university, because he defended neo-Nazis with dubious evidence. He didn't yield and instead moved further to the right, for example, with his 1980 book *Mémoire en Défense*. In it Faurisson denied the existence of gas chambers and defended himself against those who accused him of falsifying history. The book made him better known because the foreword was written by Noam Chomsky, a professor of linguistics and philosophy and a well-known opponent of the American policy in Vietnam. Chomsky's introduction caused a sensation because he declared that he would defend freedom of speech everywhere and at all times, even if Faurisson was an anti-Semite or a fanatic pro-Nazi. Of course, Chomsky received a lot of criticism, but he was used to that.

Three Lawsuits in Germany

Following this, there were two similar suits in Germany, both ending in acquittal. In July 1978, E. Schönborn, the chairman of the extreme right-wing *Kampfbund der Deutsche Soldaten* (Combat league of German soldiers), distributed pamphlets outside Anne Frank schools in Frankfurt and Nuremberg. These pamphlets stated, among other things, that the diary of Anne Frank is "a forgery and the product of a Jewish anti-German atrocity propaganda campaign intended to support the lie about the six million gassed Jews and to finance the state of Israel."

According to the judge, Schönborn had acted within the law because he had not denied human rights to any Jews. Schönborn was therefore acquitted. According to a Dutch paper (*De Volkskrant*), the judge did not exonerate Schönborn, but a sentence for defamation could only follow upon charges being filed by those personally affected.

The second case took place in Stuttgart. A former Hitler Youth leader, Werner Kuhnt, who after the war was chief editor of the extreme right-wing monthly magazine *Deutsche Stimme*, was charged with incitement of the people and defaming the memory of a dead person. In the October 1979 issue, Kuhnt had written that the diary was "a forgery" and "a fraud," not written by Anne but the product of a "collaboration of a New York scriptwriter and the girl's father." Kuhnt was acquitted by a higher court because no charges had been filed by third parties.

After performances of *The Diary of Anne Frank* in Hamburg in February and March of 1976, a pamphlet titled *Best-Seller—Ein Schwindel* (A fraud) was handed out. The contents repeated the Meyer Levin allegation. The person responsible for the distribution was Ernst Römer (born in 1904). He was found guilty of libel and fined 1,500 DM. During his case, a sympathizer of the defendant, the journalist Edgar Geiss (born in 1929), distributed pamphlets in the courtroom—these also alleged that the diary was "a fraud." Geiss's sentence was more severe than Römer's because he already had several previous convictions for similar complaints. When Geiss also appealed, the regional court decided to hear the Römer and Geiss cases jointly. There followed a repetition of what had occurred thirty years before in Lübeck: Experts were again brought in.

The Dubious Role of the German Bundeskriminalamt
(BKA: Federal Criminal Investigation Bureau)

The *Bundeskriminalamt* (BKA) in Wiesbaden was charged with preparing an expert opinion on whether it was possible "by an examination of paper and writing material to establish that the writings attributed to Anne Frank were produced during the years 1941 to 1944." The BKA visited Otto Frank in Basel to examine the material. This was a limited task, but even within these limits, the judicial researcher managed to make plenty of mistakes. In a report of a mere four pages, the BKA came to the conclusion that the types of paper used, including the covers of diary 1, 2, and 3 as well as the types of ink used in all three diaries, were all manufactured before 1950–1951 and could therefore have been used during the stated period. On the other hand, it was determined that "some of the corrections made subsequently on the loose pages [...] were written in black, green and blue ballpoint ink. Ballpoint ink of this type has only been on the market since 1951."

The report didn't indicate on which pages the ballpoint corrections were found or how many there were, a curious omission. In itself, this was a less-than-sensational report, which did not touch upon the authenticity of the diary as such. But that wasn't true for the way *Der Spiegel* treated it. On October 6, 1980, the weekly published a long article with the introductory paragraph in bold letters: "Proved by the Bundeskriminalamt: *The Diary of Anne Frank* was edited at a later date. Further doubt is therefore cast on the authenticity of that document."

The rest of the article was just as suggestive. The journalist had not wondered when the ballpoint writing had been made on the loose sheets, what the nature of these corrections was, or whether they had been incorporated in the published texts. Instead of using *Korrecturen* (corrections, or revisions) as used in the BKA report, he used the weightier term *Einfügingen* (insertions, or additions).

Der Spiegel referred to the 1960 report by the graphologist Becker, which stated that everything had been written by Anne, and that was therefore incorrect because of the use of ballpoint ink. *Der Spiegel* added, "Now if the handwriting of the original entries matched that of the additions, then there must be an impostor at work," but then added that nowadays, graphology was no longer taken very seriously. It wasn't until the end of the article that there were some quotes from the BKA report, which was where the term *Korrecturen* was used. Before that, however, the reader was told that the published diary had been subjected to countless *Manipulationen* (manipulations). *Der Spiegel* did point out that those who had doubted the authenticity of the diary had used this as an argument to deny the persecution of the Jews.

The article attracted a great deal of interest outside Germany because *Der Spiegel's* message seemed clear: something was wrong with the authenticity of the diary. This time it was not a rag by and for confirmed Nazis, but rather an unimpeachable liberal left-wing weekly that published this. In the Netherlands, members of the Anne Frank House announced to the press that after the war, Otto Frank had asked his assistant, Kleiman, to make some minor corrections to the manuscript, but these had only been clarifications.

Otto Frank was no longer able to defend himself against the accusations in *Der Spiegel,* since he died in August 1980 at his home in Birsfelden near Basel.

Because of the above-mentioned attacks on the authenticity of Anne Frank's diary, the RIOD, which had inherited Anne Frank's manuscripts, decided to publish a critical edition. Her first and second diary would be published in it for the first time. The Forensic Institute of the Ministry of Justice would research the handwriting, the paper used, the ink used, and so on. Of course, the BKA was asked for clarification, and the same researcher who in 1980 had found green and blue ballpoint ink in Anne's diary couldn't find this again five years later. The BKA didn't offer an explanation and clearly didn't care that neo-Nazis now asserted that the BKA had "proved" Anne Frank could not have written the diary. Requests to the BKA to make a pronouncement about the diary were in vain, and even political pressure in Germany was unproductive. In 2004, the NIOD (previously RIOD) did receive a significant BKA delegation, but that too was fruitless. First of all, the delegation pretended to be unaware of the report the Forensic Institute had published in the 1989 German translation of the Dutch critical edition, *De Dagboeken van Anne Frank.* In addition, the delegation didn't want to add anything to the findings of their report.

However, two years later, in June 2006, some Nazis in the eastern part of Germany near Magdeburg publicly burned a copy of the diary. After a sympathizer referred to the BKA report, this institution could no longer remain silent and issued a press release stating that its 1980 report "cannot be used to cast doubt on the authenticity of the diaries." The ballpoint ink was no longer mentioned; twenty-six years later, it was clear that the BKA still didn't want to admit that the research in 1980 had been shoddy.

The previously mentioned process against Geiss and Römer didn't resume until 1989 when the German translation of the Dutch critical edition, *De Dagboeken van Anne Frank,* was published. This translation was now used as evidence of the authenticity of Anne's diary, and Geiss was sentenced to a light fine. Geiss's lawyer appealed to the court of cassation, and one of the arguments hit the mark. The law of the press determined that a punishable offense that had been committed by means of printed matter was covered by a six-month statute of limitations. After ten years, it was no longer possible to determine when Geiss had distributed the pamphlets, and therefore the case was dismissed. The law had run its course, but this time, too, the result was far from satisfactory. Because of his poor health, the eighty-one-year-old Römer did not appeal.

Vrij Historisch Onderzoek (Free Historical Research) in Belgium

Faurisson's book had meanwhile started to assume a life of its own, and in 1991, it was published in Belgium by *Vrij Historisch Onderzoek* with the title *Het "Dagboek" van Anne Frank: een kritische benadering* (The "diary" of Anne Frank: A critical approach). The Belgian Holocaust denier, Siegfried Verbeke, had added his own *Objections to the RIOD edition*, but this focused on the betrayal. Verbeke sent his book, mostly unsolicited, to numerous libraries in the Netherlands. This time, the Anne Frank House and the Anne Frank Foundation sprang into action. They started a civil suit against Verbeke and his organization, *Vrij Historisch Onderzoek*. Both the Anne Frank House and the Foundation claimed that the defendant had acted wrongfully by doubting the authenticity of the diary of Anne Frank, and they applied for an injunction on the distribution of the book in the Netherlands on penalty of a fine of twenty-five thousand guilders.

In 1998 the district court in Amsterdam concluded that Verbeke was at fault: "Also considering the harsh, often derogatory and offensive tone of [. . .] the comments." He was no longer allowed to distribute his book in the Netherlands. The question is, of course, what the court would have done if Verbeke had challenged the authenticity in respectable terms. Two years later, the court decided in an appeal that the distribution was unlawful but didn't pursue the matter of the authenticity of the diaries.

The attacks continue, and now the internet has become the most important medium. Since Anne Frank already gets more than seven million hits on Google each year, it is obvious that an effective check on what appears about Anne is practically impossible. Moreover, anonymity plays a large role on the internet so that for the Anne Frank House or others, it is impossible to effectively counteract internet attacks against the authenticity of the diary.

Diaries of Anne Frank, the "loose sheets," and her "Verhaaltjesboek" and "Mooie zinnen boek" (© Anne Frank Fonds)

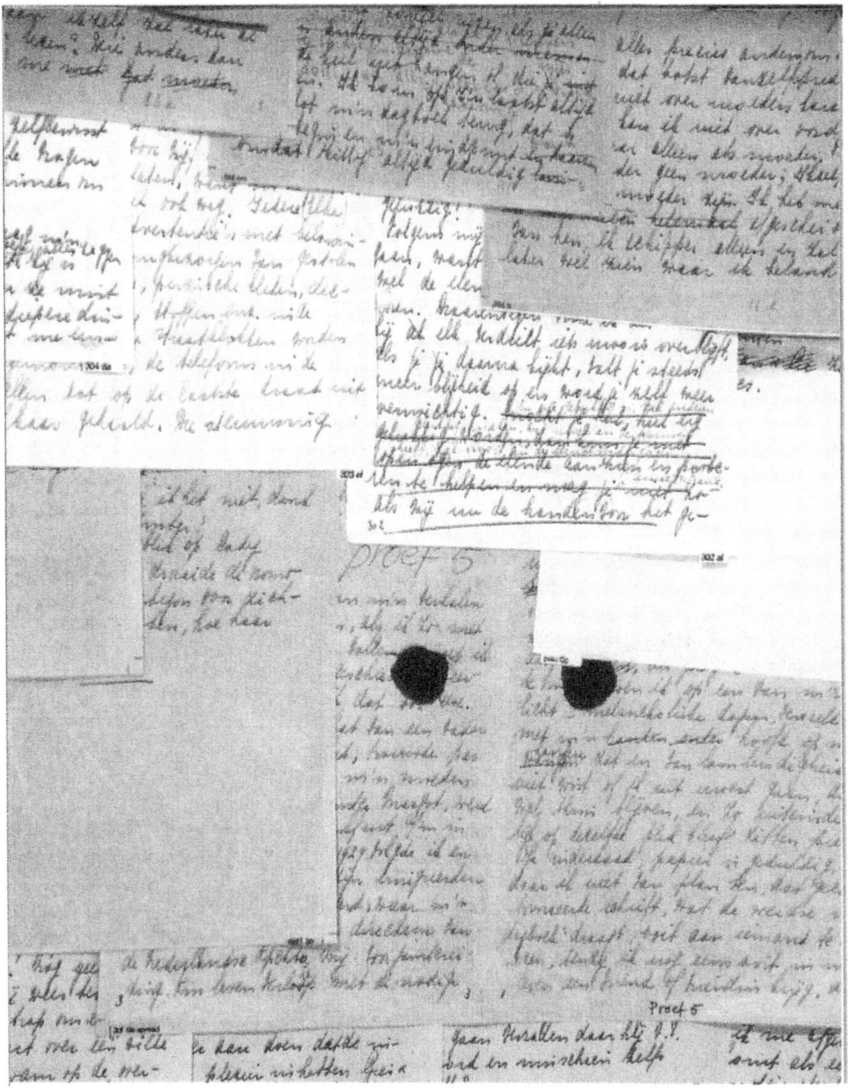

Handwriting of Anne Frank (© Anne Frank Fonds)

Advertisement in the playbill of *The Diary of Anne Frank* (October 5, 1955)

Cort Theatre

138 West 48th St. Theatre Co. Inc.

THE · PLAYBILL · A · WEEKLY · PUBLICATION · OF · PLAYBILL · INCORPORATED

Beginning Wednesday Evening, October 5, 1955   •   Matinees Wednesday and Saturday

IN THE EVENT OF AN AIR RAID ALARM REMAIN IN YOUR SEATS AND OBEY THE INSTRUCTIONS OF THE MANAGEMENT.—ROBERT E. CONDON, DIRECTOR OF CIVIL DEFENSE.

KERMIT BLOOMGARDEN

presents

JOSEPH SCHILDKRAUT

in

THE DIARY OF ANNE FRANK

Dramatized by FRANCES GOODRICH and ALBERT HACKETT

with

GUSTI HUBER

DENNIE MOORE   JACK GILFORD   CLINTON SUNDBERG

and

SUSAN STRASBERG

Directed by GARSON KANIN

Production designed by BORIS ARONSON

Costumes by HELENE PONS

Lighting by LELAND WATSON

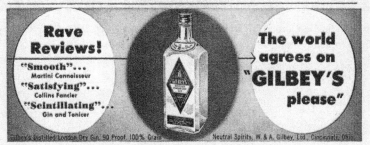
Playbill of *The Diary of Anne Frank* (October 5, 1955)

Left to right: Shelly Winters, Martin Luther King, Coretta King, and Julie and Harry Belafonte (opening night, *The Diary of Anne Frank*, April 1959) © gettyimages

Left to right: film director George Stevens, Millie Perkins (in the role of Anne Frank), and Otto Frank (1958). Dutch National Archives/The Spaarnestad Collection /Photographer unknown

Wreaths placed at the Anne Frank House on behalf of the film director and actors. Former Resistance fighters form the guard of honor (April 16, 1959). Dutch National Archives/The Spaarnestad Collection /Photographer unknown

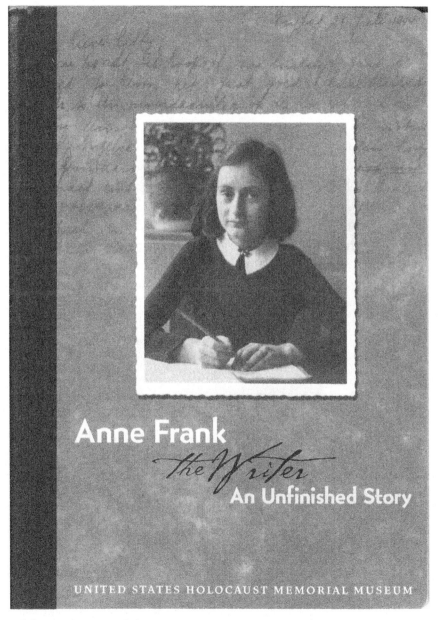

Anne Frank
~the Writer~
An Unfinished Story

UNITED STATES HOLOCAUST MEMORIAL MUSEUM

Exhibition of *Anne Frank the Writer*. In USHMM, June–September 2003.

6

Who Owns Anne Frank?

UNTIL OTTO FRANK'S DEATH IN 1980, there seemed to be a clear image of Anne Frank in the world. On the one hand, it was shaped by the compilation of her diaries by Otto Frank, and on the other hand by the American play. Meyer Levin tried to put his stamp on Anne's person by making a stage version in which Anne became a religious girl with Zionist ideals. Otto Frank didn't care for that, and his stage-daughter ultimately became a universal, idealistic teenager, who was the victim of discrimination, hate, and persecution but who continued to believe in the goodness of people. The diary itself was soon used for educational ends, to teach children to become articulate citizens in a democratic world.

The International Youth Center of the Anne Frank House, established in 1957, was a long-cherished dream of Otto Frank. Between 1960 and 1970, it was involved in creating a better world. National and international conferences alternated; dialogue was most important, and subjects such as "anti-Semitism and racism" were recurring themes for discussion. During summer conferences, participants lodged in a student apartment on Westermarkt. Its own "Anne Frank Academy" where youths would be trained was too ambitious a goal, and things never went beyond short-lived initiatives. The "historical" Anne or the writer Anne was not really important; instead it was Anne's influence on the present and the question of how her appealing ideas could be used.

The historical aspect of Anne was shown in *Anne Frank: Spur eines Kindes* (*The Footsteps of Anne Frank*) by the German author and playwright Ernest Schnabel. He tried to reconstruct Anne's life from beginning to end, from Frankfurt to Bergen-Belsen. From a heroine, he turned her back into a girl, a child. Schnabel interviewed more than forty witnesses for his book, including Otto Frank and the helpers. Some of the interviewees were asked for the first time to talk about Anne. For example, one interviewee had encountered Anne in Westerbork and reported that she was happy there— not by herself, but together with Peter. The book, published in 1958, a year and a half after the German premiere of the play, became a hit in Germany. People there talked about "guilt" in the fifties, but that was only about the guilt of the top Nazis. Schnabel addressed his book to young Germans, the ones who had spontaneously placed flowers in Bergen-Belsen after seeing the play: pilgrimages of "innocents" as penance for their parents. More than 100,000 copies of *Anne Frank: Spur eines Kindes* were sold, and it was translated into ten languages.

There is no complete Dutch translation. Instead, *Het korte leven van Anne Frank* (The short life of Anne Frank) was published in 1970 by Contact; it included *Het Achterhuis*, five of her stories, and the last four chapters of *Anne Frank. Spur eines Kindes* that covered the time from the arrest in August 1944 until April 1945 in Bergen-Belsen. Readers in the Netherlands got to read only a part of the book, but not, for example, how things had been in Westerbork. This didn't bother Schnabel, for he ended the explanation of his choice of passages from the book as follows: "The following pages contain the truth, the whole truth, and nothing but the truth." Unwittingly, he also had a scoop that would have a great impact thirty years later: In Amsterdam he had seen a home movie of a family's 1942 marriage, which shows seven seconds of Anne moving. It is interesting to note that Schnabel had been a navy officer during the war, and *Door nacht en nevel* (Through night and fog), a book by him, had been published in 1943 by the Dutch Arbeiderspers, which at the time was run by the Nazis.

Schnabel's approach was used again thirty years later by the Dutch movie director Willy Lindwer with his documentary (and book) *The Last Seven Months: Women in the Footsteps of Anne Frank.*

The short documentary *Het wonder van Anne Frank* (The miracle of Anne Frank) by another Dutch movie director, Jan Vrijman (1925–1997), was shown on television in 1959. It explored the reactions to her diary and their symbolic value. In addition to several people involved in the original publication, Otto Frank also speaks, although it was quite an effort to convince him to do it. Later, Vrijman would call this documentary "a youthful lapse."

Looking Back after a Quarter Century

The book *Weerklank van Anne Frank* (1970) (Responses to Anne Frank), compiled by Anna G. Steenmeijer, shows the reflections of the preceding years as well as the changing cultural climate. Some of the chapter titles reflect this: "The Diary as a Challenge to Educators," "What Young People Wrote," and "The Diary in American Schools." The Anne Frank worship in the making is clearly noticeable in the chapter about Anne in poetry: "We were weak/we didn't want to see the evil murder around us but the child was stronger than Herodes, than the death in Belsen," or "We will read her diary/until the coming of the Messiah." Cantatas and requiems with the Anne Frank theme started to become popular. The book also showed the great international influence of Anne Frank for which the International Youth Center, according to Steenmeijer, would have to play a central role.

In the Netherlands, there were fifteen schools with the name Anne Frank in 1970; Germany was a close second with ten Anne Frank schools; Israel was notable with twelve children's homes that carried her name. Of the almost one hundred seventy thousand people who visited the house on Prinsengracht, approximately one hundred thousand came from the United States, while only sixteen thousand Dutch took the trouble to visit the Annex that year. The Holocaust series wouldn't be shown on American television until ten years later.

During these first decades, there were barely any questions in the developments around Anne Frank, even though Meyer Levin was tireless in his attempts to promote his Anne Frank vision. The world-renowned Vienna-born Jewish psychologist Bruno Bettelheim was a notable critic who dismissed going into hiding. In 1960 he wrote the essay "The Ignored Lesson of Anne Frank" in *Harper's Magazine*; in it he accused Otto Frank and other Jews who went into hiding of a "ghetto mentality" that was inherent in Jews in the Diaspora. According to Bettelheim, these Jews closed their eyes to the approaching horror and were therefore unable to fight the Nazis and instead crawled into a hiding place. There they would be found sooner or later and then be murdered. According to him, Otto Frank was an example of this; after all, he went into hiding with his entire family in a self-created ghetto. "If they'd had a firearm, Otto Frank would have been able to shoot at least one or two members of the Grüne Polizei who came to get them." This is undoubtedly well-meant advice, but unrealistic and naïve, as was the notion that even using a butcher's knife would have been useful.

However, Bettelheim's analysis in this often reprinted essay doesn't take the local circumstances into account at all. How could one call Otto Frank and his family's departure for the Netherlands passive? And the belief that the Netherlands would remain neutral, as it did in the First World War, was widespread. Even in 1940–1941, Otto Frank made attempts to leave the country and to immigrate to the United States. When Hitler invaded the Netherlands, the Frank family was also trapped. Their second flight, to the hiding place at Prinsengracht, can't be characterized as inaction. If they could have found a boat, they would have been able to flee to Great Britain. And if they'd had the right contacts, they potentially could have reached Spain or Switzerland. But these solutions were just as dangerous as hiding in the Netherlands. Bettelheim himself fled to America just before the outbreak of the Second World War, after being in Buchenwald and Dachau for almost a year. But this doesn't make him a survival expert; his essay is a theoretical opinion, written without knowledge about the Netherlands during the occupation. Bettelheim's "hiding is wrong" corresponds to what Shelley Winters heard at the film festival in Moscow in 1962—in this case, you don't fight fascism by going into hiding.

The GDR (East Germany) Embraces Anne Frank

Although the Soviet Union ignored Anne Frank, in the GDR there were efforts to move her into the anti-Fascist camp. In the GDR, the play was performed at the same time as the performances in the German Federal Republic where it had made a profound impression. It was only then that *Das Tagebuch* appeared as a book in the GDR because Otto Frank had blocked its publication until that time. Several schools in the GDR would get Anne's name, but the farmers and workers state wanted to make an anti-Fascist documentary about Anne. The first plans for this movie, with the working title *Anne Frank und ihre Mörder* (Anne Frank and her killer), were made in 1957 in the DEFA studios in East Berlin. The Dutch movie director Jorens Ivens was involved in it as well as Lin Jaldati, who was also Dutch but living in East Berlin. She was Jewish and had been in Bergen-Belsen with Anne and her sister, Margot. It was supposed to be a solid propaganda movie. The young director Joachim Hellwig visited Otto Frank, the RIOD, and the Film Museum in Amsterdam. When it turned out that there was no movie material about concentration camps available in the GDR, a request was made to the film archives in Moscow. After 1945, the Soviet troops had taken a lot of movie material from before and during the war back to Moscow. There was no response to this request, so Hellwig went to Moscow as many as four times without success—and the last time, he was told that they didn't feel like helping make a movie aimed against Germany, because things were going so well economically between the two countries. The DEFA didn't give in easily. Walter Ulbricht, the secretary-general of the governing political party and the most important person in the GDR, wrote a letter to the Central Committee of the Communist Party of the USSR. Ulbricht listed which film material the DEFA needed. This intervention from above was fruitful in view of the original material in the resulting documentary. At the end of 1958, the movie *Ein Tagebuch für Anne Frank* opened, of course after approval of the *Filmkontrolle*, which was satisfied and determined that the "clerical-militaristic character" of West Germany was clearly shown.

The opening scene shows a young actress, who reports elatedly that she will play the role of Anne in the play *The Diary of Anne Frank*. She wants to know more about Anne and the things that Anne had not been able to write down. This is followed by photographic images of roundups in Amsterdam preceding the February strike in 1941 and images from an already known Westerbork movie with the deportation train to Auschwitz.

Despite the original boycott by Moscow, there are shots from the days after the liberation of Auschwitz and Bergen-Belsen: crematoria and stacks of bodies. Extensive attention is given to the perpetrators of these crimes, a number of whom were now living comfortably in the Federal Republic of Germany. In addition, the movie shows German companies that were involved in concentration and death camps. According to the movie, these companies were not obstructed in any way in the Federal Republic of Germany.

Anne Frank herself is barely mentioned in the documentary, but that doesn't matter because its message is loud and clear: *Wer am Krieg verdient, der hat Interesse am Krieg* (Those who profit from the war have an interest in the war).

The Communist Party in the Netherlands wanted to use *Ein Tagebuch für Anne Frank* in the elections, but it would have to be approved by the Dutch board of film censors for public showing. At first, they approved the movie for viewers eighteen years and older, but the chairman did not agree and asked for a reevaluation. The chairman thought it was "a matter of public order" and the movie has a role in "making sure that 'the man in the street' is not misled by the tempting but extremely dangerous voice of Communism that is always trying to undermine and bury the West with all imaginable means." The chairman also informed his fellow directors "that a hundred movies with Brigitte Bardot are not as bad as this documentary." A majority agreed with the chairman even though Brigitte Bardot and Anne Frank are very seldom compared. The movie was forbidden for public viewing and would therefore be shown only at closed party meetings.

Japan and Anne Frank

Another good and early example of "Anne Frank for individual use" is in Japan, where the diary appeared on the market in 1952, translated from English. Right away, there was great interest in it. By many outside Japan, this was related directly to the victimization of the Japanese, where the two atom bombs were central. In her master's thesis for Erasmus University in Rotterdam, Daphne Wesseling shows that it had been a more complicated process, especially because several translations followed one after the other. The first translations were directed to an older audience interested in the war and the aftermath. In the eighties and afterward, the translation was intended for younger girls and teenagers, and the war context was left out. In total, more than four million copies of the Japanese translation of *Het Achterhuis* were sold in Japan. The Japanese are among the most faithful visitors of the Annex on Prinsengracht. In two notable matters, Japan differs from other countries where Anne Frank is known. First, in Japan, menstruation was called "Anne's day" by girls because there was no adequate word for it in Japanese—either out of shame or modesty. As a result, there were even tampons named "Anne" on the market for a while. Second, a Protestant denomination, the Sei Iesu Kau, was so deeply impressed by Anne Frank's diary that they established an "Anne's Rose Church," later followed by a Holocaust Education Center.

Social Criticism on Prinsengracht

In the Netherlands, until the end of the sixties, the Anne Frank House had concentrated on fostering dialogue between young people from many countries who worked optimistically on building a better world during international conferences. Training programs in Dutch society were directed partially to working youth, and the Anne Frank House emulated this because, through young people, a better society would be created, not by dialogue but through confrontation. In their 2010 history of the Anne Frank House, Van der Lans and Vuijsje called this "From Esperanto to social criticism." This approach was not without problems, and the administration of the Anne Frank House didn't always agree with the more radical staff. At the beginning of 1969, an internal conflict inside the Anne Frank House between being a place of pilgrimage or a training program became apparent. The visitors came for Anne Frank and her diary, but the staff felt that this wasn't the only thing they should take away from their visit. The message they received was more important than Anne herself. They received almost no information about Anne but were increasingly confronted with exhibitions about racial discrimination and other present-day injustices. During this left-leaning period in the Netherlands, the Anne Frank House also joined in and was reproached for being "ultra left." For example, the British embassy was annoyed at an English anti-apartheid poster in an exhibition; an Israeli delegation was angry because Amnesty International in the Anne Frank House took notice of the Israelis shooting down a Libyan airplane; South Africa was angry about an exhibition that exposed Nazis in South Africa. All these reproaches urged the Anne Frank House to limit itself to the lot of Anne and the other murdered Jews. That was impossible in the political-cultural climate of the time. But these kinds of reproaches didn't noticeably influence the growth of the number of visitors.

In 1976, three years after the Yom Kippur war, there was agitation about the Dutch Palestine Committee. The Reformed Church Youth Council from Amsterdam wanted to hold a meeting in the Anne Frank House to which the Palestine Committee was invited but where the Israel Work Group was not welcome. The argument that the Reformed Church Youth Council had only rented the space and Anne Frank had nothing to do with it was not convincing for the outside world. The management, the board of trustees, and the staff all had different opinions about this question, but it was possible to settle the problem this time.

More than twenty years later, in 1998, the Palestinian leader Yasser Arafat, with the mayor of Amsterdam, honored the house on Prinsengracht with a visit. For a long time, the attitude of the Anne Frank House with respect to the state of Israel remained a sore point. Even though its statutes stated that the Anne Frank House supported the Jewish desire for their own state "as realized historically in the state of Israel," it didn't identify itself a priori with the politics of that state. People in Israel were aware of this, and it was evident in a 1977 article in the *Jerusalem Post*, which declared that the Anne Frank House was managed by the ultra-left. Seven years later, this accusation was repeated in the Netherlands by the then secretary of agriculture, Ad Ploeg, who characterized it as a "crypto-Communist organization." The agitation was enormous, the Anne Frank House reacted quite indignantly, and Prime Minister Lubbers declared solemnly that the cabinet regretted the statements of the secretary.

During the sixties and seventies, Anne Frank had clearly become more than the girl of the diary or the play. She had become a symbol that inspired the fight against evil in the world. You could actually compare her to the Dockworker statue. That statue of a robust longshoreman was erected to commemorate the 1941 February strike in Amsterdam and is the place for the annual commemoration of that strike. But in the sixties, seventies, and eighties, this statue by Mari Andriessen often served as the departure or arrival point for various demonstrations: against the regime of the Greek colonels, the Chilean general Pinochet, Dutch housing shortage, and anti-Semitism in the Soviet Union.

In 1979 the German Federal Republic issued a stamp on the fiftieth anniversary of Anne's birth. This stamp, with a serious Anne Frank, led to questions in the Dutch Lower House, such as why did the Netherlands not have an Anne Frank stamp? The Dutch postal service didn't have such a stamp on its list but changed its mind, and in 1980, a stamp was issued with a cheerful and lively Anne Frank pictured. This was done on the thirty-fifth anniversary of the liberation of the Netherlands, but Anne had to share the honor with a stamp that portrayed the Allied food drops of April 1945.

After Otto Frank's Death in 1980

The year 1980 is crucial in dealing with Anne Frank because that's when her ninety-one-year-old father died on August 19. It was only then that the general public learned that, in addition to the Anne Frank House in Amsterdam, the Anne Frank Foundation, established by Otto Frank, had been in Basel for years. The Foundation collected the worldwide copyright proceeds from Anne's diary, play, and movie, but it had never been involved with Anne's intellectual inheritance—something that would soon change.

Otto Frank had bequeathed Anne's diaries and all other writings to the Netherlands State Institute for War Documentation (RIOD), passing over the Anne Frank House. And on top of that, the RIOD—in this case the Dutch state—also became the owner of all the objects that Otto Frank had given on temporary loan to the Anne Frank House during the previous decades. These items were on an eighty-four-page list. Otto had never talked about the contents of his will, but one can speculate about the possible reasons why the Anne Frank House did not appear in his testament. He'd seen with sorrow that his pet project, the International Youth Center, was never developed, and the Anne Frank House had taken a turn to the left. Additionally, he probably feared that the number of visitors would drop; he couldn't foresee that the visit to 263 Prinsengracht would experience a dizzying growth. In 1980, the year of his death, there were 336,000 visitors, and ten years later, there were 647,000. What would have happened if the visits had diminished and the Anne Frank House had been liquidated? Would all the possessions, including Anne's diaries, have been sold to the highest bidder?

Otto Frank knew Louis de Jong, the former director of the RIOD, and in 1971 Otto had already sent some documentation about his daughter to the Institute. He probably assumed that a national institute like that would take good care of his bequest, and that the Kingdom of the Netherlands would certainly not sell the diaries. Moreover, at that time, the Anne Frank House did not yet have air-conditioned archives or a qualified archival staff. The RIOD, which would publish the complete works in 1986, had suddenly become a participant in preserving Anne's history, as was Miep Gies, who took over Otto Frank's role as interpreter of the hiding history. Seven years after Otto Frank's death, she published *Anne Frank Remembered: The Story of the Woman Who Helped to Hide the Frank Family.* Her message was: "It's up to us, all the ordinary people in the world, to make sure that this will never happen again." She would speak about Anne Frank and the others in hiding in many countries.

Eight years after the war, Otto Frank married Elfriede Geiringer-Markovits. She helped him for decades in answering the many letters that he received from all over the world. She always remained in the background, even after Otto's death. The opposite was true for her daughter Eva, who—like Anne—was born in 1929. In Great Britain, where she lived, she slowly became known as someone who had known Anne before she went into hiding and had even been her friend. In that capacity, she was prominently present at the 1986 London opening of the exhibition *Anne Frank in the World 1929–1945*, which had been created by the Anne Frank House. In this way, the Anne Frank House validated Eva's claim on Anne. In 1988, she published the book *Eva's Story: A Survivor's Tale by the Step-Sister of Anne Frank*. The very title was problematic, for she was at best Anne's posthumous stepsister; the Dutch title, *Memories of a Jewish Girl*, was more restrained. A protest against Eva's claim had already been voiced to the Anne Frank House by Jacqueline van Maarsen, who claimed to be "Anne's best friend." It became a rewarding subject for the press: two ladies fighting for prestige and respect as Anne's true friend. In 1990, Jacqueline van Maarsen published *Anne and Jopie: Living with Anne Frank*; this was followed by more publications to the same effect. Several years later, they buried the hatchet, and after that, Eva and Jacqueline often shared a stage in the Netherlands and abroad to talk about their special relationship with Anne Frank.

Where at one time Otto Frank had been Anne's only representative, now there were ever more parties and agencies that claimed Anne, at least partially. This led inevitably to a number of conflicts and collisions, for it would never be possible to establish who really spoke or wrote on Anne's behalf.

More Research about Anne Frank

At the same time as these forms of "appropriation," there was also a growing interest in the historical context of Anne Frank because of the success of her diary. Starting in the eighties, an increasing scholarly interest in the Holocaust emerged in the United States that was also directed at Anne Frank. People studied Anne's influence on American culture, and, as previously mentioned, the 1959 movie received a lot of attention. When the Holocaust established its place in the United States through Holocaust institutes and museums, there were complaints about "Americanizing the Holocaust." According to these complaints, this would lead to trivializing; an example of this was the adaptation of Anne's diary for stage and film. One of the first who expressed this clearly was Alvin H. Rosenfeld in his article "Popularization and Memory: The Case of Anne Frank" (1991). In his 1991 study *The End of the Holocaust*, he again pays attention to Anne Frank and remarks correctly that during the last fifty years, we have seen different Annes, and this development hasn't ceased. When *The Diary of Anne Frank: The Critical Edition* appeared in 1989, it was possible for people in the United States to see that Anne had written more than *Het Achterhuis*. Unfortunately, in the 1995 English Doubleday/Viking edition for general readers, one cannot see the difference between Anne's early, often immature style, including grammatical errors, and her rewritten version, which is much more mature. In the English translation, that distinction has disappeared; no grammatical errors are to be found, and Anne's language and style from 1942 are the same as in 1944 so that one can't follow her progress in writing. That's almost unavoidable—how would one translate Dutch grammatical errors?

Because the two versions of the diaries could now be seen, a debate started about which one should be considered the real diary. Laureen Nussbaum, who, as a half-Jew, fled from Germany to the Netherlands where she met the Frank family, feels that the diary rewritten by Anne is the "real" version. According to her, Anne would have wanted to publish that version, and that's why version B should be published as the final diary. Nussbaum and others fail to consider the possibility that Anne might have done something quite different with her rewritten diary. It's a guess, but it's not strange to suppose that Anne, if she had survived, might have looked at her diaries in a different way, completed them, or perhaps thrown them away.

In *Reading Anne Frank as a Woman* (1993), the historian Berteke Waaldijk showed to which literary influences Anne was exposed. In addition to her schoolwork and the "adult" books she read while in hiding, there is also the important influence of Cissy van Marxveldt (1893–1948), the well-known writer of girls' books, including the "Joop ter Heul" series. A number of names used by Anne come from this series, as in her diary entry of September 28, 1942: Pop, Kees, Emilie, Connie, Bobbel, and others. We see that Anne frequently praises the books of this author in her diary.

A feminist point of view gave still another perspective on Anne Frank. In 1996, Denise da Costa wrote her doctoral dissertation on Anne Frank and Etty Hillesum, focusing attention on Anne's feminine side. Anne is almost always full of praise when writing about her father and his great influence on her. Da Costa wanted to show that his influence on Anne's thinking and writing is less significant than is generally assumed. Anne's writing "in spite of oppression," like Etty Hillesum's writing, is characterized as resistance against the German oppressor. Until she was deported to Auschwitz, the fifteen year older Etty Hillesum had also kept a diary that was published and appeared in translation. In addition, there is an Etty Hillesum Center, and, just like Anne, she has faithful followers, although she hasn't yet become a worldwide phenomenon of Anne's magnitude.

In her book *Writing as Resistance: Four Women Confronting the Holocaust*, Rachel Feldhay Brenner characterizes writing despite oppression as the most important characteristic of Anne's diary. In the book, she points out similarities and differences between Edith Stein, Simone Weil, Anne Frank, and Etty Hillesum.

The use of Anne's diary by Holocaust deniers was explained by Deborah Lipstadt in *Denying the Holocaust: The Growing Assault on Truth and Memory* (1993). She shows how, as discussed in chapter 5, the Frenchman Faurisson had become an intermediary between Europe and the United States and how this "intelligent denier" of the authenticity of Anne's diary was a welcome guest at "revisionist" conferences in the United States.

The hopeful message and the goodness of mankind were described as utopianism by Barbara Chiarello in her article "The Utopian Space of a Nightmare: The Diary of Anne Frank" (1994). Obviously, Anne Frank also appears in the "memory" mania of recent years. James Young devotes a short chapter, "The Anne Frank House, Holland's Memorial 'Shrine of the Book,'" to this aspect in *The Art of Memory* (1994). He places the house on Prinsengracht in the "National Memorial Traditions."

Lawrence Graver was one of the first to make use of archives in his examination of the play: the Meyer Levin Collection and the Kermit Bloomgarden Papers in Boston, and the Goodrich and Hackett Papers in Madison. In *An Obsession with Anne Frank: Meyer Levin and the Diary* (1995), Graver concluded that Levin's first version of the play in 1952 was closer to the original diary than Goodrich and Hackett's version. Levin makes her more like the realistic author of the *Diary* (she writes easily of "talk, whispers, fear, stink, flatulation, and always someone on the pot") than the sanitized heroine created by Goodrich and Hackett. Unfortunately for Levin, his script was not considered sufficiently theatrical, particularly by professionals clinging to conventional ideas about Broadway plays.

In *The Stolen Legacy of Anne Frank: Meyer Levin, Lillian Hellman, and the Staging of the Diary* (1997), Ralph Melnick, who did extensive archival research like Graver, was also of the opinion that Levin's version was closer to the original diary. He was more critical of Lillian Hellman's activities. As a Communist (he liked calling her a Stalinist), she had done all she could to "de-Semitize" the play, and Otto Frank had approved. Melnick mentions almost casually that Hellmann received a check of $10,000 from the Soviet government months after the Broadway premiere. Whereas Graver's Levin tilts mournfully at windmills, Melnick turns him into a courageous fighter for Jewish values that were suppressed in the fifties. Until then, the Americans, especially Goodrich and Hackett, had been blamed for "de-Semitizing," "Americanizing," and "universalizing" the diary for the stage, but Melnick now took Otto Frank to task. He was one of the first to show the great influence of Otto Frank on the realization of the play.

The Dutch-American author Ian Buruma also concentrated on the play in "The Afterlife of Anne Frank" in the *New York Review of Books* (February 19, 1998). In his opening sentence, he stated: "Anne Frank was an ambitious young woman, and most of her wishes came true." But he was of the opinion that if you blame the Hacketts for "de-Semitizing" the Frank family, you could blame Levin for making them "too Jewish." A strong attack on Otto Frank came from the writer Cynthia Ozick, who right before the premiere of the revamped play *The Diary of Anne Frank* wrote an extremely critical article in *The New Yorker* (October 6, 1997) with the title "Who Owns Anne Frank?" In the article, she argued that it might have been better if Anne's diary had disappeared and that so many people have tinkered with Anne's diaries that Anne is no longer visible. According to Ozick, Anne was no longer recognizable, and that could be blamed partially on her father.

Five Diary Sheets with Revelations

The year of the "new" play, 1997, was also the year of new revelations concerning Anne Frank. Until then, there was only Schnabel's *Anne Frank Spur eines Kindes* (*The Footsteps of Anne Frank*) about her life, but that was from 1958, and Schnabel had used some anonymous sources. Now, forty years later, two new biographies have been published about her: *Anne Frank: The Biography* (updated in 2014) by the Austrian journalist Melissa Müller; and *Roses from the Earth: The Biography of Anne Frank* by the British journalist Carol Ann Lee.

The first book had the support of Miep Gies, the one-hundred-year-old helper of those in hiding, and the second book had the equally heartfelt support of Bernard "Buddy" Elias, Anne's cousin and the president of the Anne Frank Foundation in Basel. Lee continued her research, and four years later, she published *The Hidden Life of Otto Frank*. Both authors had done a lot of research in archives and had interviewed many people.

Melissa Müller received important information from Cor Suijk, who had worked in the Anne Frank House for many years and had become the international director of the Anne Frank Center in New York. Even more interesting was the fact that he had functioned as confidant of Otto Frank for many years. In that capacity, he turned out to have in his possession five of Anne's still unknown diary sheets, something that he had carefully kept secret. It was a new beginning of the diary on a loose sheet, with the front and part of the back written on. The most exciting line is " and I will take care that no one will get it [the diary] in his hands." It was undated, but it was most likely in May 1944 that Anne started rewriting her diary; therefore, it must come from that time frame. In addition, there was a large sheet, folded in two—three sides of which are written on. These three pages are dated February 8, 1944, and that date corresponds to the diary entry in her first version. The three pages caused much excitement and led to a court case, feverish deliberations, and the transfer of a large sum of money. The first lines read: "As I seem to be undergoing a period of reflection at the moment and letting my mind range over everything and anything, my thoughts have naturally turned to Father and Mother's marriage. It has always been presented to me as an ideal marriage. Never a quarrel, no angry faces, perfect harmony, etc., etc. I know a few things about Father's past, and what I don't know, I've made up." This is followed by a rather unflattering description of the marriage.

The compilers of the critical edition knew this description of the marriage because it also occurs in Anne's A, or first, diary version. In 1986, the Anne Frank Foundation in Basel did not give its consent to include this passage, and a footnote of the critical edition stated: "In the 47 crossed out lines Anne gives an extremely unkind and partly incorrect picture of her parents' marriage. At the request of the family this passage has been deleted."

There was no B version of this passage, but that wasn't too odd, for in her rewritten diary, Anne left things out from time to time. Also, it wasn't obvious that some loose sheets were missing.

Cor Suijk's story was that Otto Frank didn't want the investigator from the BKA who came to Basel to do research (see p. 67) and to see this passage about the marriage. That's why Otto Frank had removed the loose sheet and given it to Cor Suijk. This sounded rather absurd, since the investigator could read the same story in the "A" version. After the visit of the BKA expert, Otto Frank had supposedly indicated that Cor Suijk could keep those pages, something that also seems quite absurd. Almost twenty years later, Cor Suijk let himself be convinced to publish these diary entries, partly because Otto Frank's widow had died in 1998. Melissa Müller would have the scoop and include these "new" passages in her book "in order to fill in Anne's family history with an essential mosaic tile," according to Suijk.

When the Anne Frank Foundation found out about this forthcoming publication, it prohibited printing these diary pages because it would mean a violation of the copyright. The Anne Frank House was of the opinion that Cor Suijk had received these sheets in his function as a staff member. Consequently, after almost twenty years, he would have to hand them over to the Anne Frank House. The NIOD suggested that they first check whether the sheets were authentic. If so, these sheets would be included in the next printing of the critical edition, *De Dagboeken van Anne Frank*. After an examination, the sheets indeed turned out to be written by Anne.

In the meantime, a newspaper (*Het Parool*) had printed the sheets, and as a result, the paper was served a temporary injunction by the Anne Frank Foundation. Everyone could now see what Anne had written, but readers often overlooked her remark, "and what I don't know, I've made up." At any rate, the court ruled against the Foundation.

Meanwhile, Cor Suijk, now president of the Contemporary Holocaust Education Foundation in New York, was willing to hand over the sheets to the NIOD, but that would have to be in exchange for some money. The original idea had been that Cor Suijk himself would take care of financial backing for his Holocaust Education Foundation, but that didn't work out. The Ministry of Education, Culture, and Science made an agreement with Cor Suijk and Christie's auction house in New York, where the pages were stored for the time being. This renowned auction house had set the value of the pages at $1.2 million and would also look for financial backing, an odd activity for an auction house. If no financial backing could be found, the Kingdom of the Netherlands would transfer 10 percent of the estimated value to Suijk's American education foundation. At one point, Suijk reported that he'd already received a bid of $10 million from an unknown dealer, but that led nowhere. The Kingdom of the Netherlands clearly didn't want a lawsuit about such a delicate question and bought off the conflict, not with $120,000, 10 percent of the estimated value, but with $300,000.

In this way, in March of 2001, the minister of education, culture, and science, Loek Hermans, received the fifth edition of *De Dagboeken van Anne Frank*, an edition that included the dearly paid pages that were now stored securely in the safe of the NIOD.

It was striking that a Dutch ministry was willing to pay so much for Anne's work, for at the time there wasn't much interest in Anne Frank in the Netherlands. This ministerial behavior showed that people were becoming more sensitive about national patrimony, but it can also illustrate that Anne was becoming more Dutch at the end of the twentieth century. That was revealed very nicely during the 2004 KRO television broadcast "The Greatest Dutch Person of All Times" when Anne ultimately—after all the fuss around her nationality—ended up in eighth place, something that would have been impossible ten years earlier. Three years later, the United States copied this appropriating behavior when a representative from Long Island proposed making Anne Frank an honorary citizen of the Unites States. Doing so would make Anne the seventh in a list of prominent figures like Winston Churchill and Mother Teresa. This American attempt to incorporate Anne was the result of the discovery of a number of letters from Otto Frank from 1940 and 1941. Her citizenship was supposed to be a kind of compensation because the American immigration authorities had refused Frank at the time. This attempt to obtain honorary citizenship failed because of insufficient support.

Individual Appropriations

After "state appropriations" by the Unites States, the GDR, and the Netherlands, there were, of course, individual appropriations as well.

What about Nelson Mandela? One would think that this world-famous South African, the recipient of more than 250 domestic and foreign honors, wouldn't need Anne Frank as a symbol. In Johannesburg in 1994, Mandela opened the exhibition *Anne Frank in the World* and recounted that he and his comrades in the Robben Island prison gained inspiration from those "who challenge injustice even under the most difficult circumstances." Mandela then mentioned that his fellow activist Govan Mbeki said, "Some of us read Anne Frank's Diary on Robben Island and derived much encouragement." Another time, Mandela said that "some" (of his comrades) had read the diary, and then again he claimed that he'd read the diary before he was imprisoned, and later that he'd read it in prison.

The former mayor of Amsterdam, Ed van Thijn, recounted in a television program that Anne's diary had been smuggled page by page into all the cells of Robben Island. However that may be, much strength was derived from the diary for the struggle against apartheid. The Anne Frank House used Mandela's remarks to spread Anne's message more widely. Since 2008 there has been an Afrikaans translation of *Het Achterhuis*: *Die Agterhuis*.

Less known is the Anne Frank connection of the Dutch culinary author, Berthe Meijer, who published *Leven na Anne Frank* (Life after Anne Frank) in 2010. Anne appears exactly once in the book, in an implausible scene in Bergen-Belsen. Early in 1945, then seven-year-old Berthe saw that the older girls were encouraged to tell stories to the youngest children to cheer them up: "One of these girls was Anne Frank, who could barely stand. She was skin and bones and her voice was a whisper. With a horse blanket around her, she sat there and told us fairy tales."

It wasn't the first time that Berthe Meijer told this story. When filmmaker Willy Lindwer interviewed eyewitnesses for his prize-winning documentary *The Last Seven Months of Anne Frank* (1988), Berthe Meijer was one of the eyewitnesses. In the interview, she describes the just-quoted scene, but she says that it wasn't until her return to the Netherlands that she realized the girl reading fairy tales had been Anne Frank. Meijer had mentioned Anne earlier, for in the *Literaire Eetboek* (1985), she had gathered twenty-five "literary" recipes: "Here is a recipe of potato cholent [of Anne Frank] that fortunately contains meat. It would have been a feast for them."

The Bezige Bij, the same publisher that published *Life After Anne Frank*, also published the already mentioned *Vogelvrij. De jacht op de Joodse onderduiker* (Outlawed: The hunt for Jews in hiding) by Sytze van der Zee. Although less than one-fifth of the book is about the betrayal of Anne Frank, Anne's photo adorns the cover. The most extreme and perhaps the most tasteless example of appropriation is by the Swedish writer Barbro Karlén, who in her book *En de wolven huilden: fragmenten uit een leven* (And the wolves cried: Fragments from a life) claimed that she had been Anne Frank. Even if you believe in reincarnation, this book still is no more than commercially hitching a ride on Anne Frank's name.

The Anne Frank House

From its establishment in 1957, the Anne Frank House played a large role in the meaning, interpretation, and explanation of Anne Frank. Naturally, a phenomenon involves commotion; this was also true for Anne. Fifty years after the Annex was opened to the public, *Het Anne Frank Huis. Een biografie* was published. It offered a remarkably critical look into half a century of Prinsengracht 263, inside and outside. The book was commissioned by the Anne Frank House, which, strikingly, left authors Van der Lans and Vuijsje total freedom. Furthermore, until then, the Anne Frank House had always shown a distinct tendency to control what others wrote or said about Anne or the Anne Frank House. The year 2010 was also important because the Anne Frank House could proudly announce that it had received all of Anne's manuscripts on semipermanent loan. How that happened after Otto Frank had bequeathed them to the RIOD thirty years earlier will be set forth later in this chapter.

During the first years, it was quite difficult for the Anne Frank House to collect enough money to preserve 263 Prinsengracht in some way and to open it to the public. The mayor of Amsterdam, Van Hall, made an appeal in newspapers to donate money, and this brought in 200,000 guilders. After discussions with the University of Amsterdam and the city, a more structural solution was found: Anne's house and the neighboring house would be saved, and around the corner, on Westermarkt, a student house would be built. In addition to money from the Netherlands, money came from Germany; at the end of the sixties, the German state and the city of Frankfurt contributed more than 150,000 marks.

German generosity was also evident in an undertaking by Volkswagen, for in 1959, the Volkswagen importer donated the proceeds from the 10,000th and 10,001st Volkswagens imported into the Netherlands to the Anne Frank House. At the time, there were still many Dutch who, because of the German occupation, refused to ride in a German car, let alone buy one.

The same year, a statue of Anne was erected in Utrecht, which was presented by that city's youth; it was the first of many Anne Frank statues and busts in the Netherlands and abroad.

In 1960 the Jewish standup comic and humorist Max Tailleur gave an "Anne Frank" medal to a secretary who had helped him during a tour of South Africa. It wasn't the Anne Frank House that protested the awarding of this (joke) medal but the former Resistance—which, by the way, didn't protest Tailleur's performing in the county of apartheid.

In the spring of 1963, Otto Frank visited Pope John XXIII, who indicated that he had read the diary.

In 1967 the Anne Frank House had its tenth anniversary and announced that it would like to start an "Anne Frank Academy where international political training and international psychology will be taught." This was postponed because of the Six-Day War in Israel, and the academy didn't get off the ground. Otto's dream would not be realized.

Anne also fell prey to commerce. At the end of 1967, a record about Anne Frank ("with the rhythm of the beat") was released. Everyone immediately cried out against it, so this catchy tune was taken off the market. The seventeen-year-old singer was so shocked by all the commotion that she stopped making recordings and later stopped doing performances.

As already mentioned, toward the end of the sixties, as elsewhere in Dutch society, sociopolitical training and politics inside the Anne Frank House became more important than international youth contacts. But toward the end of the eighties, it underwent an important change of direction that again mirrored the sociopolitical changes in society. Activism seemed to be past, and under the direction of the new director Hans Westra, 263 Prinsengracht became a modern museum where the staff is engaged in education rather than politics. However, that change didn't happen without internal struggles, and it also led to casualties: Joke Kniesmeyer was dismissed after representing the Anne Frank House to the public for years. Now the emphasis was on Anne herself, her history, and also on what she still had to say to the world. This led to a series of exhibitions that toured the world—exhibitions that showed the history of Anne Frank, Nazism, and anti-Semitism, and also called for a better world. The Anne Frank House was always very proud when an exhibition took place in a former dictatorship— Chile, Argentina, or South Africa—because their citizens could learn much from Anne's ideas and perhaps better themselves. Using Anne Frank's story as a teaching method in British jails or visits to the Annex from tough American ghetto youths were presented as examples of the positive effect of her diary. There wasn't much evaluation.

An increasing number of Anne Frank productions were performed with varying success. The Anne Frank House and the Anne Frank Foundation gave opinions about such productions less often than previously. The Royal Ballet of Flanders produced a musical *Je Anne* (Yours, Anne) with a Dutch premiere in Amstelveen, just outside Amsterdam. No one was offended by the idea of a musical, but public interest was minimal. When eight years later another Anne Frank musical was staged, this time in Spain, the cartoon drawn by Collignon in a newspaper (*De Volkskrant*) was outspoken: "After the success of Anne Frank the Musical; part II: Bergen-Belsen the Musical?" The Anne Frank House was very positive about the musical, but Buddy Elias threatened legal action. It didn't come to a complaint or a lawsuit since no literal quotes from Anne Frank had been used in the musical.

In 1995, fifty years after liberation, there was a professional performance of the third Anne Frank play, this time with the singer Boudewijn de Groot as Otto Frank. He had to compete against the memory of Jeroen Krabbé, who had been brilliant in that same role ten years before. The ballet and the play had the approval of the Anne Frank House, but that wasn't the case for a Japanese animated cartoon about Anne, which the Anne Frank House judged to be "too fairy tale-like."

At the end of 1994 and in early 1995, the Anne Frank House took a stand against the KRO television program *Reporter* that was preparing a broadcast about it. KRO had found out that the Anne Frank House had a seven-second amateur film, a unique film with the only moving images of Anne. This film was deposited at the Anne Frank House but was the property of the NIOD/Kingdom of the Netherlands, and the copyrights had been arranged ambiguously. KRO wanted to use the movie images, but it turned out that the Anne Frank House had sold the exclusive rights to the British filmmaker Jon Blair, who was making a documentary about Anne. *Reporter* wanted to find out about the ins and outs of the Anne Frank House, which didn't like that. Then, like private detectives, staff members of the Anne Frank House followed the people with whom *Reporter* had sought contact, and all this was documented. *Reporter* was able to get hold of a complete file with discussion reports and became angry about these investigative practices. For his documentary, *Anne Frank Remembered*, Blair received an Emmy. Three years later, it turned out that the film fragment in question was a copy because, according to a statement by the Anne Frank House, the original had been lost years ago.

In 1996, it became obvious that the Anne Frank House in Amsterdam and the Anne Frank Foundation in Basel were at odds. The Anne Frank House had registered the brand "Anne Frank" worldwide so that it was the only one who could use the brand. The Foundation in Basel was upset about that and wanted to have the intellectual property of the Anne Frank brand in Switzerland as well. Going to court didn't help the Foundation, however; the Anne Frank House could prove that the Foundation had never done anything with the Anne Frank brand except collect royalties and transfer money to humanitarian projects. Apparently, the Anne Frank House was not included in those donations, considering the small sum that the Foundation allotted to the major renovation of the house on Prinsengracht at the end of the twentieth century. Less than four hundred thousand guilders came from Switzerland, although a million had been requested. The money needed, around ten million guilders, was collected in many ways and by many parties.

The Renovation of the Anne Frank House

The twentieth century was concluded by the festive opening of the totally renovated Anne Frank complex by Queen Beatrix and her husband, Prince Claus. Richard von Weizsäcker, the former president of the Federal Republic of Germany, gave a speech.

It is a miracle that the house on Prinsengracht from 1645 hadn't already collapsed, crashing, with the more than ten million visitors who had walked through the front of the house and the Annex. It became a radical restoration, renovation, and new addition project, but some of the neighbors didn't care about Anne Frank's reputation. They were against the lines of visitors at the canal and made it clear that they were fed up with the noisy demolition and building activities. The student house on Westermarkt was demolished; instead there came office space and a visitors' cafeteria. Both the Annex and the front part of the house were restored in such a way that visitors would feel that they were back in the original structure. "Back to then" was very important, but the original furniture was not reinstalled; that would be in the way of the stream of visitors, and if it had been, the number of one million visitors a year (starting in 2011) would certainly not have been possible.

The house at 263 Prinsengracht was—and remained—a place of pilgrimage where Anne had experienced and written down everything in her diary, but the Anne Frank House also provided information and education. The information included details about racial discrimination, the persecution of the Jews, hiding, what happened to those in hiding, and what happened to Anne's diaries after the war. In 2011, for example, there was an interactive educational exhibition *Free2Choose* about conflicting basic rights in which many matters were formulated in a less categorical way than in the past.

After restoring 263 Prinsengracht, the Anne Frank House tackled the next project: the residence of the Frank family on the third floor at 37 Merwedeplein. In partnership with the Ymere housing corporation, this building was brought back to its original state and was also given a new use. The Amsterdam Refugee City Foundation was invited to use the residence to house a writer who "is persecuted or threatened, or is obstructed as a writer" in his own country. It's debatable whether it's appealing for a threatened writer to stay in a house with such unpleasant memories. Some years later, the apartment was quite run-down, and there was also a fire.

Outside Amsterdam there was also work to be done. After all, Anne had spent some time in transit camp Westerbork. All that was left of the camp was the villa where the German camp commander Gemmeker had lived. There are extensive plans to conserve it; a glass dome over the villa would prevent further deterioration. For the rest, the camp terrain is a barren plain, where some time ago a cement camp block in a "ruin-type" style was constructed. But the public wanted more, so the hunt was on for original camp barracks, which in the early seventies had been sold to neighboring farmers for next to nothing. They no longer existed, except for one, and it unfortunately burned down in 2009. That just happened to be the barracks in which Anne and Margot, among many others, had been forced to work— a real Anne Frank barracks. The board of Westerbork Memorial Center had planned to place the barracks back in Westerbork, but that was no longer possible. They now considered using replicas in which pieces of the original wood were incorporated.

There was a lot of news around Anne Frank, who was not only elected number eight as the "Greatest Dutch Person of All Times," but who also received first place from the *Historisch Nieuwsblad* (Historical newsmagazine). Her diary, not the writer, was central in the sixty-year anniversary celebration of the publication of *Het Achterhuis* in 2007. The NIOD and the Anne Frank House worked together smoothly on this.

That year there was also news from New York, from the YIVO Institute for Jewish Research. Three letters from Otto Frank from 1941 had been found in their archives, among them a letter to his old friend Nathan Strauss, in which Otto tells him that he wants to emigrate to the United States with his family and asks Nathan for help. It had been known for decades that Otto wanted to emigrate, but YIVO treated it as big news. The discovery of these letters led to a short discussion in the United States about the callous behavior of the American government in taking in very few Jewish refugees even before the United States was in the war.

The Chestnut Tree

The greatest excitement during the first decade of the twenty-first century concerned the "Anne Frank tree." In a garden bordering the Annex stood a more than 150-year-old chestnut tree that no one would have heard of if Anne had not written about it three times. On February 22, 1944, she wrote: "The two of us [Peter and Anne] looked at the blue sky, the bare chestnut tree glistening with dew, the seagulls and other birds glinting with silver as they swooped through the air."

The leafless chestnut tree had slowly become "a tree of remembrance" or "the tree that saw everything." By 1993 the tree was severely affected by soil pollution and was in danger of dying. The city council of Amsterdam was willing to spend as much as three hundred thousand guilders on it after a councilman appeared on a CNN camera and said the city would save the tree. This, and later the contemplated radical renovation of the house on Prinsengracht, caused criticism. The first plans for the substantial expansion of the Anne Frank House caused a revolt among the neighbors. It was an example of "not in my backyard" behavior, but there was also an undercurrent that Anne Frank was for the tourists and not for the neighborhood. The local residents didn't want to be bothered by the tourists. The *NRC Handelsblad* essayist Max Pam expressed this in his piece "The Mausoleum of Anne Frank" in which he proposed that tourists should make appointments by telephone—then these lines of waiting visitors would simply disappear. His article was an expression of general criticism and not focused on a specific political issue as had been the case in the eighties.

Ten years after the municipal rescue, the tree appeared to be back on the verge of death. In 2004, there seemed to be sufficient evidence that there was no way to save the tree, which suffered from dying trunk rot and a "fulminating infestation of a bracket fungus." After consultation with several tree specialists, the inner-city district was advised to have the tree cut down to prevent it from falling. Anyone who thought that the Anne Frank House would want to preserve its Anne Frank tree because of its emotional value was wrong. People in the Anne Frank House were for cutting down because there was a real danger that in a powerful storm the chestnut tree would crush the Annex in its fall—which was not an enviable prospect, certainly if it happened during the museum's opening hours. The owner of the building at 188 Keizersgracht in whose garden the tree stood was also for cutting down, as the tree could fall on his house with a different wind direction.

When the report of the tree's approaching death became known nationally and internationally, there was great agitation. The famous Anne Frank tree now seemed to be of invaluable meaning and had to be saved at any expense. Actually, this was predictable; In Amsterdam trees seem to be practically holy, and now a tree could be defended with the help of Anne Frank herself. In the words of a former editor of the ex-resistance paper *Het Parool*: "The cold indifference to the extent of our past in the war reaches a low point with the tree-felling permit for the Anne Frank tree." Even the words "with this Anne Frank is again betrayed" were uttered. There were many protests, especially from Germany, a country with an almost mythical tree and woods tradition.

Suddenly, numerous tree doctors from home and abroad came and opined that the tree was perhaps slightly sick but could certainly remain upright with a little help. Most of the neighbors also demanded that the tree should stay, whereby they ignored the fact that very few people could see the Anne Frank tree; after all, it stood in the garden of an enclosed block. People even went to court to prevent the cutting, and rescue plans were busily proposed. Dozens of TV crews were present at a "pulling" test to see how much the tree could stand. A "Support the Anne Frank Tree" foundation was established, and a lot of money was collected with a benefit gala. Then, a steel construction was designed to keep the tree in its place. Contractors were approached to carry out the needed work at cost or for less. In April 2008, an eight-meter-high steel corset was placed around the tree, and everyone seemed happy, although it looked absurd. Meanwhile, "real" Anne Frank chestnuts were offered for sale on the internet; it seemed that $700 had already been offered. But in the summer of 2010, its time had come. Just after noon on Monday, August 22, the thirty-ton tree toppled—fortunately into the garden. While care had to be taken to keep cutting and chestnut looters away, pointing out the culprits started soon. The designer was no good, the steel was no good, or the welding construction was inferior. A contractor, who had at first helped free of charge, now wanted to be paid, and members of the tree foundation board started to accuse one another.

Meanwhile, saplings of the "tree of life" have started growing everywhere, so that in time, various Anne Frank trees will be competing to see which is the most authentic.

What Is Where?

The contents of Otto Frank's will seemed clear but would still lead to conflicts. It came as a big surprise in 1980 that Otto Frank had bequeathed his daughter's diaries, her "favorite quotes notebook," her "book of tales," her postcards, and other items to the NIOD (then RIOD) in his will, not only for the NIOD, but especially for the Anne Frank House, which was already the administrator of many hundreds of objects having to do with Anne. Over the years, the Anne Frank House had received those on loan from Otto Frank, who in his will transferred these objects to the NIOD on the condition that they would remain in the Anne Frank House. Through a use agreement, the NIOD saw to it that the Anne Frank House could continue to exhibit the diaries and diary entries for visitors. The copyright of Anne's manuscripts and the extensive photo collection remained in the hands of the Anne Frank Foundation in Basel.

This photo collection consists of four photo albums, put together by Otto Frank, who also took most of the photos. According to the will, three albums were the property of the NIOD and one, the property of the Anne Frank House. That album had been delivered anonymously to the Anne Frank House in the seventies. Next to all the photos in these albums there is a claim that the copyright is held by the Anne Frank Foundation, but there are also photos that were obviously not taken by Otto Frank, like Anne's school photos and the small photos made in a photo booth. The Anne Frank House treated these photos as if it owned them; this became apparent during the photo exhibition *Noordzee, een keuze uit de fotocollectie Nederland* (North Sea, a selection from the Netherlands photo collection) in the Nieuwe Kerk in Amsterdam from August to October 2000. A photo of Margot Frank on the beach from one of the NIOD photo albums was displayed, but the caption only stated "Anne Frank House." This caused the NIOD to discuss matters with the Anne Frank House, which, as a result, promised to mention the NIOD as the owner if a photo from the NIOD collection was used.

Just as during the seventies the Anne Frank House had become the owner of a photo album from an unknown source, in a similar way the NIOD had become the owner of seven until then unknown Anne Frank objects: two letters, three photos, a small pendant, and a French grammar. Günther Schwarberg, an editor at the German weekly *Stern*, contacted the NIOD in the spring of 1981 and said these items had come to him and the weekly but that they would be donated to the NIOD. Unfortunately, the identity of the previous owner could not be revealed. After the transfer of the Anne Frank objects, an extensive article with illustrations appeared in *Stern* on May 21, 1981. Two weeks later, the weekly published a letter to the editor from Buddy Elias, Anne's cousin and president of the Anne Frank Foundation. In this letter, he corrected a photo caption—that was all. More than twenty years later, Buddy Elias claimed these *Stern* items because, according to him, they had been stolen from the Frank family and had great emotional value. When and by whom these had been stolen was not clear, and it appeared that the theft had never been reported. The NIOD presented the matter to Minister M. J. A. van der Hoeven of the Ministry of Education under whose authority the NIOD fell at the time. Van der Hoeven in turn sent the matter to the advisory committee for restitution requests of items of cultural worth and Second World War (Restitution Commission). However, the commission didn't get around to a substantive judgment about the affair, for after devoting a few considerations to succession questions (April 26, 2006), the commission wrote:

> Before coming to the question of which person or institution can be considered as (original) party entitled to the seven aforementioned matters, the commission shall have to judge if it is competent to come to a substantive judgment in this matter. Pursuant to article 2 of its establishment decree, the task

of the commission is limited to cultural goods over which possession was lost though circumstances that had a direct connection with the Nazi regime. . . .

In view of the aforementioned facts, which in no way indicate loss of possession during the Second World War but on the contrary indicate a loss of possession that took place in the nineteen eighties, the answer to the question posed under 4 must be that any connection between the loss of possession and the Nazi regime is lacking. Despite indications of involuntary loss of property, the commission will have to abstain from a judgment about the ownership claim of Mr. B.E.

The ball was now back in the court of the minister who, surprisingly, decided to honor the request of Mr. Elias and grant the objects to the Anne Frank Foundation in Basel. The press release of the ministry explained this as follows: "Despite the fact that the commission in its opinion declares itself unqualified about the lack of connection between the loss of property in the nineteen eighties and the Nazi regime, the results of the examination served for the minister as a recommendation to return the *Stern* artifacts."

It is much more likely that it wasn't so much "the results of the examination" that were decisive for the minister as the general political sensitivity concerning plundered Jewish possessions. It was for a good reason that the Restitution Commission was set up by the government at the end of 2001—this commission was to be in charge of a "generous restitution policy." The NIOD prepared to transfer the objects to the Anne Frank Foundation in Basel, but that wasn't necessary, since the Foundation had already given the objects on loan to the Anne Frank House in Amsterdam.

It wouldn't be the last time that a minister would be occupied so directly with Anne Frank, as is shown in the way that the loan would be arranged.

The Anne Frank House was never happy with the fact that the diaries and other Anne Frank manuscripts had been bequeathed to the then RIOD by Otto Frank and were deposited at the NIOD. The NIOD was mentioned without enthusiasm at the Anne Frank House—the words "will" and "property" are not used: "After Otto's death in 1980, at his request all manuscripts of his daughter were transferred to the Kingdom of the Netherlands, which in turn placed the National Institute for War Documentation (then still RIOD, later NIOD) in Amsterdam in charge of this bequest."

Who actually owned what had no influence on the exhibition policy in the Annex, because clear agreements had been made about different responsibilities. To combat the deterioration of the material as much as possible, every trimester, another loose sheet was laid down, or a page of the first diary was turned to prevent discoloration.

In 2002 the result of an important project was announced. There now were facsimiles of the manuscripts by Anne Frank, including her diaries, loose sheets, the Book of Tales, and the book of favorite quotes. The project, led by Pau Groenendijk of the Amsterdam workshop *Mooie Boeken* (Beautiful books), had led to an astounding result: It was impossible to distinguish the facsimiles from the originals. These facsimiles were made in case the diaries were irretrievably damaged. Moreover, the original diaries no longer needed to be taken out for scholarly research, and the Anne Frank House now was less dependent on the NIOD. One copy remained in Amsterdam, and a second one went to the Anne Frank Foundation in Basel; both organizations also used the facsimiles in exhibitions.

After the renovation of the building on Prinsengracht, where air-conditioned storage vaults had been installed, the Anne Frank House continued the project. The entire manuscript collection would be best stored on Prinsengracht and exhibited when possible. Van der Lans and Vuijsje summed it up nicely: "For years it had been the ardent wish of the Anne Frank House, but the relations with NIOD, the diary administrator, were difficult. Ultimately the minister of Education had to become involved in order to get things moving." It was, of course, an advantage that the chair of the Anne Frank House Supervisory Board was of the same political party as the minister. The NIOD received the order that all of Anne Frank's manuscripts had to be transferred to the Anne Frank House on semipermanent loan. There were numerous preconditions, but the Anne Frank House had reached its goal of exhibiting most of Anne Frank's manuscripts. The NIOD remained responsible for the management. A commission established by the Royal Netherlands Academy of Arts and Sciences (KNAW), which NIOD falls under, has advised NIOD and the Anne Frank House since that time so that preserving and exhibiting at Prinsengracht is done with the necessary care.

The agreement between the NIOD/KNAW and the Anne Frank House was signed on June 11, 2009, the evening before the eightieth anniversary of Anne's birth. Minister Ronald Plasterk of the Ministry of Education was elated: "Anne Frank is world famous, and it's fantastic that the Dutch public as well as the world public can now for the first time see her complete work in the original, and moreover in the house where it was written." Director Marjan Schwegman of the NIOD said about the agreement: "The story of her life will draw more attention and therefore make a greater impression thanks to this new agreement." Director Westra of the Anne Frank House stated: "It is fantastic that the diaries are 'coming home' after many years, back to the place where they were written."

A year later, on March 18, 2010, the manuscripts left the NIOD. The institute seized that moment to show the international character of Anne Frank. Among others, the ambassador of Germany, the mayor of Amsterdam, and the ambassador of the United States were present on this occasion. Five weeks later, the manuscripts were exhibited for the first time in the Anne Frank House, on its fiftieth anniversary.

A Girls' Book or Literature?

THE EDITORS OF THE CRITICAL edition of the diary have sometimes been reproached for not remarking on the name Kitty, the person to whom Anne addressed her diary: "Scholars have long ignored the fact that Anne Frank in her diary with her letters to Kitty chose a character from Joop ter Heul books. They didn't know the books by Cissy van Marxveldt" (Monica Soeting in *Letterhoeke* 2008, number 2). This last is partially true, since the editors of the critical edition are males, who know little about girls' books. But nowhere is a literary analysis or textual interpretation done by the editors—that is left to the readers. In the critical edition, footnotes are used only when Anne writes about events outside the Annex, about bombings, for example. It is curious that literary critics didn't pay attention to Anne's texts until more than forty years after the publication of *Het Achterhuis*. Moreover, the key to the name Kitty had been present all those years. On September 21, 1942, Anne writes in her diary, "I'm enthusiastic about the *Joop ter Heul* series," and three weeks later, on October 14, she writes, "Cissy van Marxveldt is a terrific writer." The Dutch historian Berteke Waaldijk had made the Van Marxveldt connection in 1993. The critic Soeting also mentions that Otto Frank let Van Marxveldt read his daughter's diary before anyone else, but no convincing proof can be found for this story.

The published diary of Anne Frank was in the first place, and for decades, considered as a *document humain*, an *objet trouvé*, a war testimony, or a historical source, but not as literature. There was one exception, as mentioned previously; in early 1946, Kurt Baschwitz wrote to his daughter Isa: "It is the most moving document about this time that I know, and an astonishing literary masterpiece as well." Perhaps the diary was considered girls' literature, but no literary analysis was done on such literature, certainly not at the time. Anne's diary is used as a teaching tool, especially in the United States—not to examine its literary qualities, but to show how good or evil people can be. The emphasis on the play and the differences between the diary text and the play have stood in the way of a discussion about literary qualities. It is interesting, however, that in 1957, an Anne Frank literary prize was created, intended for young writers under thirty. Goodrich and Hackett, who had adapted the diary for the stage, had made $5,000 available for this. The first year's prize winners were two Dutch authors, Harry Mulisch for his novel *Archibald Strohalm*, written five years earlier, and Cees Nooteboom for his debut novel *Philip en de anderen* (*Philip and the Others*). The prize was distributed annually until 1966, but during the eighties, an attempt was made to blow new life into it. As a result, the Polish-Israeli writer Ida Fink (1921–2011) received this prize in 1985, presented by the mayor of Amsterdam.

Naming a literary prize after Anne Frank but not letting her belong to literature could be called inconsistent. The nonliterary aspect was undoubtedly the reason that the diary has almost never led to literary inspiration. Instead, dozens of musical compositions and just as many sculptures and paintings have been created. A solitary literary exception is the Jewish-American writer Philip Roth with his 1979 novel, *The Ghost Writer*.

During a 2007 symposium on the sixtieth anniversary of *Het Achterhuis*, the literary critic Arjan Peters alleged: "The abundance of Anne Frank documentation is in stark contrast to the minimal mention of the Diary in literary reference works." Thirty years earlier, the poet John Berryman (1914–1972) had already pointed out the literary aspect of *The Diary of a Young Girl*: "The work has decided literary merit; it is vivid, witty, candid, astute, dramatic, pathetic, terrible—one falls in love with the girl, one finds her formidable, and she breaks one's heart."

Perhaps Berryman was too early; for a long time, he remained a voice in the wilderness. In 1980, in *Het geminachte kind* (The disdained child), Guus Kuijer considered Anne a great writer who achieved a literary feat and wrote a masterpiece.

The publication of *De Dagboeken van Anne Frank* in 1986 created new attention for what Anne had actually written. In this critical edition of the diary, readers could follow the development of a writer, and the publication of the definitive edition of *Het Achterhuis* in 1991 led to a discussion about the literary character of Anne's writing.

In 1986, in his essay *Het meisje en de dood* (The girl and death), Harry Mulisch confessed that he had read *Het Achterhuis* just a short time before and that his first visit to the Annex on Prinsengracht had also taken place recently. He had a novel point of view by arguing that it's good that "*Het Achterhuis* doesn't really belong in the literary canon." That would play into the hands of the neo-Nazis, who would then say that *Het Achterhuis* was "a literary creation that is passed off as truth and reality." It is, of course, strange that the possible actions of neo-Nazis might influence a literary canon.

In the United States, Laureen Nussbaum had been busy promoting Anne Frank as a great writer since the mideighties. Just like the Frank family, she had fled Germany in the thirties and met the Franks in Amsterdam. More than ten years after the war, she immigrated to the United States where she finished her career as professor of foreign languages and literature. She found Anne "a most promising young writer" and based this also on the fairy tales and other stories written by Anne. Nussbaum studied the critical edition of the diary extensively and is of the opinion that version B, the version rewritten by Anne, should be published as *Het Achterhuis* because that was her ultimate version. A problem with this is that Anne did not rewrite the period between April 1 and August 2, 1944, because she didn't have the time. This is also the opinion of Gerrold van der Stroom, the co-editor of the critical edition of the diary, who has frequently emphasized Anne's authorship. He regards *Het Achterhuis* as a "literary work" and feels it is "an underappreciated book of Dutch literature"

In 1996, *Aarts' Letterkundige Almanak. Na het Anne Frank-Herdenkingsjaar 1995* (Aarts' Literary Almanac: After the Anne Frank commemoration year of 1995) was published. This time, the yearbook, which had been published since 1980, was completely devoted to writers who died during the war years 1940–1945. Anne's well-known school photo with a pen at the ready adorned the cover.

Anne's authorship was central in the small catalog that was published for the 2003 exhibition *Anne Frank the Writer. An Unfinished Story*. In honor of its tenth anniversary, the United States Holocaust Memorial Museum in Washington had organized this exhibition in cooperation with the NIOD. During discussions preceding the construction of the museum, there had been suggestions for using texts by Anne Frank in the Hall of Remembrance, but that proposal didn't receive a majority. In the 2003 exhibition, Director Sarah Bloomfield wanted to draw attention to Anne's literary side by using her diary texts frequently in the catalog. American visitors may have thought that Anne wrote fluent English, since various texts could be seen in translations that more or less imitated Anne's handwriting to give it an air of authenticity. The importance of this exhibition was emphasized even more because Laura Bush, who had been a librarian, opened the exhibition. However, her opening words had more relevance to her husband's function as president than to Anne's writing: "The impact of this exhibit extends far beyond its walls, as do the writings of Anne Frank. Her words and her courage continue to inspire us as we strive for peace in the Middle East and the world."

In 2009 Francine Prose published *Anne Frank, the Book, the Life, the Afterlife* in which she examined Anne's writing talent in more detail. According to Prose, Anne had created a "well thought out work of art . . . a literary work." The discussion of the literary character of Anne Frank's diaries has not yet subsided, but it is striking that in the Netherlands people are more restrained about using the designation "literary" than those abroad.

Anne Frank as Inspiration

The Ghostwriter, the first part of Philip Roth's Nathan Zuckerman trilogy, was published in 1979 but was set in 1956. Anne Frank, appearing as Amy Belette, a Holocaust survivor, plays an important role. The main character (Philip Roth?) falls in love with her. Was this a provocative book, trivializing the Holocaust by the writer of *Portnoy's Complaint*? Roth wrote the book in part as a protest against the atmosphere of sanctity that increasingly surrounded Anne Frank. But it was also aimed at the stage-Anne, whose Jewish identity, the reason for her death, was taken away by the playwrights. In this, he followed Meyer Levin, but Roth could defend himself behind his freedom as a man of letters. It was a one-off confrontation of this writer with Anne Frank, but she would continue to influence his life.

When the author of this book visited Roth in London ten years later, he was barely willing to talk with me about Anne Frank. Later, Roth's wife, Claire Bloom, wrote in her memoirs that Roth had a photo of Anne on his desk, next to a photo of Claire at the same age. Not only Roth, but Bloom, too, was occupied with Anne Frank; two years before the publication of *The Ghostwriter*, Bloom recorded Anne's diary as an audiobook.

It wasn't until 2005 that another literary work was published, inspired by Anne Frank. In *The Boy Who Loved Anne Frank*, the American author, Ellen Feldman, wrote about Peter, who was in hiding with Anne but survived the war and ended up in America. There he watches how his girlfriend's diary becomes world famous and how this opens the floodgates of his memory. In the positive reviews of this book, there is not a word about Holocaust trivializing, and one would think that, literarily speaking, everything was allowed if it was about the Holocaust or Anne Frank. But that turned out not to be true in view of the reactions to the 2010 young adult book *Annexed* by the British author Sharon Dogar. The British equivalent of the Anne Frank House, the Anne Frank Trust in London, felt that one should not make fiction out of Anne Frank and her hiding, but that wasn't the most serious criticism. Even before the book was published, critics fell all over the writer because in the book, Anne Frank and Peter van Daan supposedly had a more or less sexual relation. Some papers called it "Anne Frank sexed-up," and it was clear that for many this went too far. On reading *Annexed*, the book turned out to be better than expected, and the reviews were rather positive, but that made no difference. You weren't supposed to touch Anne, literally and figuratively.

8

How to Continue in the Twenty-First Century?

Anne's Image

The evolution of Anne's image is not linear, and it obviously differs from country to country. Who or what is Anne Frank? A gifted young writer, an ordinary Jewish girl who became a victim of the Holocaust, a moral guide after Auschwitz and Hiroshima? One can imagine a common denominator.

During the first years after the publication of *Het Achterhuis*, Anne Frank was primarily a Dutch symbol of Jewish suffering, and after the stage adaptation by Goodrich and Hackett, she became an (American) teenager who is having a hard time but continues to believe in the goodness of people. She is no longer exclusively Dutch but has become universal. In the United States, starting in the 1980s, Anne slowly became a Jewish victim of the Holocaust, and at the end of the twentieth and the beginning of the twenty-first century, Anne has become a bit more Dutch. The Holocaust has started to play a smaller role in the evolution of her image, but that evolution never stops. Therefore, there remain many Annes.

Anne Frank as a writer easily reached the twenty-first century. Her diary continues to be translated, and its sales continue undiminished; her place of hiding now draws more than one million visitors per year.

What is the basis of the success of the diary and the house on Prinsengracht? Because of her age, Anne did not have well-formed ideas about society, politics, religion, or life. It's almost all open, and because she can no longer explain her own writings, everyone can create his or her own image of Anne. This image is based on reading and endless interpretation of the diary that Anne wrote between June 12, 1942, and August 1, 1944, in the relatively "luxurious" but quite confining hiding place. How you view Anne depends on your nationality, race, background, gender, age, and other factors. It's a book for adolescent girls who are crazy about their father but don't think much of their mother. It stops just before the horrors reach her, and the Holocaust appears "only" in a couple of dream fragments. It's not a Holocaust book with blood on almost every page; on the contrary, during the hiding, there is laughter, love, and kissing.

Copyright

By 2015, it had been seventy-five years since Anne Frank's death in Bergen-Belsen. According to international copyright rules, the copyright on her writings expired at the end of that year. It's true at any rate for *Het Achterhuis*, which was published in 1947, but later expiration dates apply for the translations. Her original texts, versions A and B, weren't published until 1986, and copyright expiration dates for those will be counted from that date onward. Does this mean that everyone can now fabricate his or her own *Achterhuis*?

At the end of 2015, the court in Amsterdam determined that the Anne Frank House has the right to make a copy of Anne's complete texts for scholarly research. However, the Anne Frank Foundation in Basel, the copyright holder, had forbidden this and taken the Anne Frank House to court.

On January 1, 2016, a Frenchman placed the complete Dutch text of *Het Achterhuis* on his French website, whereupon the Foundation ordered him to remove it immediately.

The Anne Frank Foundation denies that the rights on *Het Achterhuis* became available at the end of 2015, and a few years ago, a new argument to lengthen the copyright was suddenly produced. The Foundation reported that numerous experts at home and abroad had determined that Otto Frank had done much more than edit his daughter's work. With his editing work, he had earned his own copyright. He had become an author alongside Anne; the word *coauthor* was avoided by the Foundation. If you add another seventy years to the date after the death of Otto Frank, you see that the Foundation will have the copyright until 2050.

The fact that deniers will say, "See, Otto Frank wrote it," doesn't seem to bother the Foundation. The fact that copyright has a limitation in years, for good reason, seems to escape the Foundation, and serious questions remain. Are they going to put together a new *Achterhuis* in fifty years? Copyright wasn't set up for that.

It looks as though more lawsuits will follow, with the lawyers profiting. It would be best for the Foundation to drop all claims and release Anne's texts now and forever. That seems to be entirely in the spirit of Otto Frank, who wanted to bequeath his daughter's ideals to the world.

What Will Happen?

More textual analysis will be done on Anne's writings, something that can be done more extensively since the 1986 publication of the critical edition, *De Dagboeken van Anne Frank*. An analysis of the development of her language can be done only with the Dutch edition, because in the English-language edition, there is no difference between her first more childish and clumsy diary entries and the more mature rewritten diary letters.

Thanks to the critical edition, it is now possible to look carefully at the differences in content between the first and second version. For example, on October 9, 1942, Anne writes: "We assume that most of them are being murdered. The English radio says they're being gassed. Perhaps that's the quickest way to die." It wasn't until the critical edition that it became evident these lines were in the rewritten version B and in the ultimate publication of *Het Achterhuis*, but not in her first diary, which means that she didn't write it until the spring of 1944 or later. Of course, that raises questions. Did she not find it sufficiently interesting to write this down in October 1942, and how could she remember that particular radio broadcast a year and a half later?

Researchers will dive into "old" material in which interviews made in the fifties or later with those involved (for example, the filmmaker Vrijman with *Het Wonder van Anne Frank*) will have an important place.

Het Achterhuis will slowly but surely be included in the canon of world literature, even though writers like Elie Wiesel and Primo Levi, to name only two, have given a more pronounced literary voice to the Holocaust.

Will Anne become more Jewish in the Orthodox sense, or Jewish in a more liberal sense? Since the beginning, Otto Frank clearly pushed Anne's Jewish side into the background and never actually reconsidered it. There are photos of Otto with numerous religious dignitaries like the Pope or with the Dominican priest Dominique Pire of the Anne Frank village for refugees, but photos with a rabbi are rare. An exception was Rabbi Jacob Soetendorp of Amsterdam, who knew Otto from before the war and was chair of the Anne Frank House during the sixties.

The "renewed" play of 1997 is a bit more Jewish, but the stage-Anne, hardly at all. If she remains exclusively a Holocaust victim, she could become more Jewish, but if Anne becomes a more universal victim of all suffering, that certainly won't happen.

The copyright expiration at the end of 2015 could also lead to far-reaching commercialization, whereby publishers produce small, easily manageable Anne Frank books for different types of schools. Ever more versions of *Het Achterhuis* will be created that will possibly be at an increasing distance from the original manuscripts. This last will certainly be fodder for neo-Nazis, who will claim that the diary is a flagrant forgery.

The House on Prinsengracht

Is growth still possible for the more than one million visitors to Prinsengracht, and if so, how? By extending opening times, more people can enter, but in the summer the house on Prinsengracht is already open until 10:00 p.m. If you make the rooms barer by not giving explanations on the walls, the visitor flow will be faster, but is that desirable? It's clear that there will be more visitors, for tourism is increasing everywhere.

The Anne Frank House will continue to grow, and it's striking that the expansion is mostly occurring abroad; various Anne Frank exhibitions can be seen annually in more than two hundred cities in dozens of countries. These exhibitions are visited by hundreds of thousands, and in every country something appropriate is added. In Argentina attention is paid to the military dictatorship of the past, and soldiers in training visit the exhibition. They will, of course, know better than to participate in a military coup. A national Anne Frank Day was declared in Argentina, and an Anne Frank monument can even be found in Buenos Aires. It's a replica of the small statue on Merwedeplein in Amsterdam. After visiting the exhibition in Soweto, youthful visitors will hopefully contribute to a more tolerant South Africa by spreading the message of Anne Frank.

The political components in the exhibitions abroad are conspicuous, but these have been absent in the Netherlands for years. After the "years on the left," there is now an apolitical period on Prinsengracht, where the emphasis is on "The House" and the internet. It can be expected that the historicizing tendency will continue. Exhibitions will increasingly show the "historical" Anne Frank, her family, the helpers inside and outside, and the surroundings of the Annex. The replica of the work barracks in Wester-bork will most likely receive an Anne Frank seal.

Gradually, the Holocaust will play a smaller role in the image around Anne. An increasing number of people connect Anne with their own story ("Anne Frank's story is my story") or the suffering of their ancestors. Anne is linked to the struggle against all the evil in the world. The 2015 television documentary *In Line for Anne Frank* shows this very well; a number of people waiting in the long line to visit the Annex were asked why they are there. A black man from the South connects Anne's lot with that of his ancestors in the struggle against racial discrimination, and two Tibetan monks see much of Anne in the Dalai Lama. In the TV documentary *De magie van het dagboek van Anne Frank* (*The Magic of the Diary of Anne Frank*), television host Astrid Joosten interviews a number of national and international public figures about Anne. The Holocaust is hardly mentioned in their answers, and Jeffrey Wright, an American actor, even tells the interviewer, "I am a survivor." The American general Wesley Clark managed to connect the NATO bombing of Belgrade in 1999 to Anne's diary.

In the twenty-first century, people are less likely to believe in the "inner goodness of people" than in the 1950s. Yet it is Anne's optimistic and lively side that will attract new readers and new visitors. The phenomenon of Anne Frank will continue on.

Bibliography

Other Sources

NIOD-press clippings
NIOD-Archive KB l-Personen Anne Frank (seven boxes)

Bibliography

Aarts, C. J., and Willy Tibergien. *Aarts' Letterkundige Almanak*. Amsterdam: C. J. Aarts, 1996.

Anne Frank 75. Bundeling lezingen ter gelegenheid van de 75ste geboortedag van Anne Frank. Amsterdam: Anne Frank Stitchting, 2004.

Avisar, Ilan. *Screening the Holocaust*. Bloomington: Indiana University Press, 1988.

Barnouw, David. "Anne Frank and Film." In *Anne Frank: Reflections on Her Life and Legacy*, edited by Hyman A. Enzer and Sandra Solotaroff-Enzer, 165–173. Urbana: University of Illinois Press, 2000.

———. "Anne Frank and Miep Gies; a Girl and a Woman." In *Holocaust Heroes: Fierce Females, Tapestries and Sculpture*, edited by Linda Stein, 27–29. Philadelphia: Old City Publishing, 2016.

———. "Anne Frank in the United States and in the Netherlands." In *Four Centuries of Dutch-American Relations*, edited by Hans Krabbendam, Cornelis A. van Minnen, and Giles Scott-Smith, 960–979. Amsterdam: Boom, 2009.

———. *Anne Frank voor beginners en gevorderden*. Den Haag: SDU, 1989.

———. "De Anne Frank Industrie; een modern Lourdes." In *De vele gezichten van Anne Frank. Visies op een fenomeen*, edited by Gerrold van der Stroom, 192–199. Amsterdam: De Prom, 2003.

———. "Een delicaat onderwerp. Film en Het dagboek van Anne Frank." In *Jaarboek Mediageschiedenis*. No. 7: 213–239. Amsterdam: Stichting Beheer IISG/ Stichting Mediageschiedenis, 1995.

———. "The Authenticity of Anne Frank's Diary." In *Twentieth-Century Literary Criticism*, edited by Jennifer Gariepy, vol. 58, 76–90. Detroit: Gale Research, 1995.

————. "The Authenticity of the Diary." In *The Diary of Anne Frank* (Bloom's Modern Critical Interpretations), edited by Harold Bloom, 5–29. New York: Infobase Publishing, 2010.

Barnouw, David, and Gerrold van der Stroom. *Wie verraadde Anne Frank?* Amsterdam: Boom, 2003.

Baron, Lawrence. *Projecting the Holocaust into the Present.* Lanham: Rowman & Littlefield, 2005.

Bettelheim, Bruno. "The Ignored Lesson of Anne Frank." *Harper's Magazine*, November 1960.

Bigsby, Christopher. *Remembering and Imagining the Holocaust: The Chain of Memory.* Cambridge: Cambridge University Press, 2006.

Bistrović, Miriam. *Antisemitismus und Philosemitismus in Japan.* Essen: Klartext, 2011.

Bloom, Claire. *Leaving a Doll's House: A Memoir.* New York: Little, Brown and Company, 1996.

Bloom, Harold, ed. *The Diary of Anne Frank* (Bloom's Modern Critical Interpretations). New York: Infobase Publishing, 2010.

Boer, Marijke de. "Onderzoeker aan het woord: Monica Soeting," *Letterhoeke*, vol. 4, no. 2 (2008), 24–27.

Brenner, Rachel Feldhay. *Writing as Resistance: Four Women Confronting the Holocaust.* University Park: Pennsylvania State University Press, 1997.

Broos, Ton J. "Anne Frank's Literary Connections." In *The Low Countries*, vol. 8, 177–189. Rekkem: Stichting Ons Erfdeel, 2000.

Buruma, Ian. "The Afterlife of Anne Frank." *New York Review of Books*, February 19, 1998, 4–8.

Chiarello, Barbara. "The Utopian Space of a Nightmare: The Diary of Anne Frank." *Utopian Studies*, vol. 5, no. 1, 128–140. University Park: Pennsylvania State University Press, 1994.

Cole, Tim. *Selling the Holocaust, from Auschwitz to Schindler: How History Is Bought, Packaged, and Sold.* New York: Routledge, 2000.

Costa, Denise da. *Anne Frank & Etty Hillesum: Inscribing Spirituality and Sexuality.* New Brunswick: Rutgers University Press, 1998.

Dogar, Sharon. *Annexed.* London: Andersen Press, 2010.

Doneson, Judith E. *The Holocaust in American Film.* Syracuse: Syracuse University Press, 2002.

Enzer, Hyman A., and Sandra Solotaroff-Enzer, eds. *Anne Frank: Reflections on Her Life and Legacy.* Urbana: University of Illinois Press, 2000.

Feldman, Ellen. *The Boy Who Loved Anne Frank.* New York/London: W.W. Norton & Company, 2005.

Fietz, Barbara F. *Editionskriterien der Leseausgabe Mirjam Presslers der Tagebücher der Anne Frank.* Magisterarbeit. Oldenburg: Carl von Ossietzky Universität, 1999.

Flanzbaum, Hilene, ed. *The Americanization of the Holocaust*. Baltimore/London: The John Hopkins University Press, 1999.

Frank, Anne. *Mooie-zinnenboek*. Amsterdam: Prometheus, 2004.

————. *The Diary of a Young Girl*. Garden City, NY: Doubleday, 1952.

————. *The Diary of a Young Girl: The Definitive Edition*. New York: Doubleday, 1995.

————. *The Diary of Anne Frank: The Revised Critical Edition*. New York: Doubleday, 2003.

————. *Verhaaltjes en gebeurtenissen uit het Achterhuis*. Amsterdam: Prometheus, 2001.

Gies, Miep, and Alison Gold. *Anne Frank Remembered: The Story of the Woman Who Helped to Hide the Frank Family*. New York: Simon and Schuster, 1988.

Goodrich, Frances, and Albert Hackett. *The Diary of Anne Frank*. Play, based on the book *Anne Frank: Diary of a Young Girl*. New York: Random House, 1956.

Idem, newly adapted by Wendy Kesselman. New York: Dramatists Play Service, 2000.

Graver, Lawrence. *An Obsession with Anne Frank: Meyer Levin and the Diary*. Berkeley: University of California Press, 1997.

Grobman, A., and J. Fishman. *Anne Frank in Historical Perspective: A Teaching Guide for Secondary Schools*. Los Angeles: Martyrs Memorial and Museum of the Holocaust, 1995.

Hellwig, Joachim, and Günther Deicke. *Ein Tagebuch für Anne Frank*. Berlin: Der Nation, 1959.

Heyl, Matthias. *Anne Frank*. Reinbek bei Hamburg: Rowohlt Taschenbuch, 2002.

Higham, Charles. *Audrey: A Biography of Audrey Hepburn*. New York: Macmillan Publishing Company, 1984.

Holland, Victor H. *Geel bloed, hardheid en bibbergeld*. Den Haag: Holland Movies, 2004.

Insdorf, Annette. *Indelible Shadows: Film and the Holocaust*. Cambridge: Cambridge University Press, 1983.

Iskander, Sylvia Patterson. "Anne Frank's Autobiographical Style." *Children's Literature Association Quarterly*, Summer 1991.

Jaeger, Toef. *Uitgeverij Contact 1933–2008. Een kleine geschiedenis*. Amsterdam: Contact, 2007.

Jaldati, Lin, and Eberhard Rebling. *Sag nie, du gehst den letzten Weg. Erinnerungen*. Berlin: Buchverlag Der Morgen, 1986.

Jong, Louis de. "The Girl Who Was Anne Frank." *Reader's Digest*, 1957.

Karlén, Barbro. *And the Wolves Howled: Fragments of Two Lifetimes*. London: Clairview Books, 2000.

Kirschnick, Sylke. *Anne Frank und die DDR: politische Deutungen und persönliche Lesarten des berühmten Tagebuchs*. Berlin: Ch. Links, 2009.

Kuijer, G. "De onderduiker." In *Het geminachte kind*. Amsterdam: De Arbeiderspers, 1980.

Kushner, Tony. "I Want to Go on Living after My Death: The Memory of Anne Frank." In *War and Memory in the Twentieth Century*, edited by Martin Evans and Ken Lunn, 3–25. Oxford: Berg, 1997.

Lans, Jos van der, and Herman Vuijsje. *Het Anne Frank Huis. Een biografie*. Amsterdam: Boom, 2010.

Lee, Carol Anne. *Roses from the Earth: The Biography of Anne Frank*. London: Penguin, 1998.

———. *The Hidden Life of Otto Frank*. London: Viking, 2002.

Leinweber, Agnes. *Anne Frank—Zur Entstehung eines politischen Mythos' in beiden deutschen Staaten* Diplomarbeit. Berlin: Freie Universität Berlin, Fachbereich Politik-und Sozialwissenschaften, Otto-Suhr-Institut für Politikwissenschaft, 2000.

Lejeune, Philippe. "Comment Anne Frank a réécrit le Journal d'Anne Frank." In *Les Brouillons de soi*, 331–365. Paris: Seuil, 1998.

Levin, Meyer. *The Obsession*. New York: Simon & Schuster, 1973.

Lindwer, Willy. *The Last Seven Months of Anne Frank*. New York: Random House, 1992.

Lipstadt, Deborah L. *Denying the Holocaust: The Growing Assault on Truth and Memory*. New York: The Free Press, 1993.

Maarsen, Jacqueline van. *My Name Is Anne, She Said, Anne Frank*. London: Arcadia Books, 2003.

Meijer, Berthe. *Leven na Anne Frank*. Amsterdam: De Bezige Bij, 2010.

Melnick, Ralph. *The Stolen Legacy of Anne Frank: Myer Levin, Lillian Hellman, and the Staging of the Diary*. New Haven/London: Yale University Press, 1997.

Miller, Judith. *One, by One, by One: Facing the Holocaust*. New York: Simon and Schuster, 1990.

Moss, Marylin Ann. *Giant: George Stevens, a Life on Film*. Madison: University of Wisconsin Press, 2004.

Müller, John. *Het literair Eetboek*. Amsterdam: De Bijenkorf, 1985.

Müller, Melissa. *Anne Frank: The Biography*. New York: Henry Holt & Company, 2014.

Nussbaum, Laureen. "Anne Frank." In *Women Writing in Dutch*, edited by Kristiaan Aercke, 513–575. New York: Garland Publishing, 1994.

Ozick, Cynthia. "Who Owns Anne Frank?" *The New Yorker*, October 6, 1998.

Polak, Bob. *Naar buiten, lucht en lachen. Een literaire wandeling door het Amsterdam van Anne Frank*. Amsterdam: Bas Lubberhuizen, 2006.

Pressler, Mirjam. *Anne Frank: A Hidden Life*. London: Macmillan, 2000.

———. "Grüsse und Küsse an alle." *Die Geschichte der Familie von Anne Frank*. Frankfurt am Main: S. Fischer, 2009.

Prose, Francine. *Anne Frank: The Book, the Life, the Afterlife*. New York: Harper-Collins, 2009.

Rensman, Eva. *De Anne Frank Stichting en haar lessen uit de Tweede Wereldoorlog 1957–1994*. Utrecht: Utrechtse Historische Cahiers, 1995.

Rittner, Carol Ann, ed. *Anne Frank in the World: Essays and Reflections*. New York: M. E. Sharpe, 1998.

Romein-Verschoor, Annie. *Omzien in verwondering*. Amsterdam: De Arbeiderspers, 1970.

Rosenfeld, Alvin H. *A Double Dying: Reflections on the Holocaust Literature*. Bloomington: Indiana University Press, 1980.

———. "Anne Frank—And Us: Finding the Right Words." *Reconstruction* 2 (1993): 86–91.

———. "Popularization and Memory: The Case of Anne Frank." In *Lessons and Legacies: The Meaning of the Holocaust in a Changing World*, edited by Peter Hayes, 243–278. Evanston, IL: Northwestern University Press, 1991.

———. *The End of the Holocaust*. Bloomington: Indiana University Press, 2011.

Roth, Philip. *The Ghost Writer*. New York: Farrar Straus & Giroux, 1979.

Rubin, Susan Goldman. *Searching for Anne Frank: Letters from Amsterdam to Iowa*. New York: Abrams, 2003.

Sagan, Alex. "An Optimistic Icon." In *German Politics and Society*, vol. 13, no. 3 (1995): 95–107.

Sarig, Roni. "Sadako Sasaki and Anne Frank: Myths in Japanese and Israëli Memory of the Second World War." In *War and Militarism in Modern Japan*, edited by Guy Podoler, 158–172. Folkestone: Global Oriental, 2009.

Schloss, Eva. *Eva's Story: A Survivor's Tale by the Step-Sister of Anne Frank*. London: Allen, 1988.

Schnabel, Ernst. *The Footsteps of Anne Frank*. London: Southbank, 2015.

Schroth, Simone. *Das Tagebuch. The Diary. Le Journal. Anne Franks Het Achterhuis als Gegenstand eines kritischen Übersetzungsvergleichs*. Münster: Waxmann, 2006.

Schwartz, Daniel. *Imagining the Holocaust*. New York: St. Martin's Griffin, 1998.

Siems, Marion. *Erläuterungen und Dokumente. Anne Frank Tagebuch*. Stuttgart: Philip Reclam, 2003.

Stam, Dineke. "Laat me mezelf zijn, dan ben ik tevreden: Anne Frank." In *Sekse en Oorlog. Jaarboek voor Vrouwengeschiedenis*, vol. 15, 153–161. Amsterdam: Stichting Beheer IISG, 1995.

Steen, Jürgen. *Anne aus Frankfurt. Leben und Lebenswelt Anne Franks*. Frankfurt am Main: Historisches Museum, 1990.

Steenmeijer, Anna G., red. *Weerklank van Anne Frank*. Amsterdam: Contact,1970.

Stier, Oren Baruch. *Holocaust Icons: Symbolizing the Shoa in History and Memory*. New Brunswick: Rutgers University Press, 2015.

Stroom, Gerrold van der. "Anne Frank's Favorite Quotes Notebook." In *The Low Countries, Crossroads of Cultures*, edited by T. J. Broos, M. Bruyn Lacy, and T. F. Shannon, 187–196. Münster: Nodus Publikationen, 2006.

Stroom, Gerrold van der, ed. *De vele gezichten van Anne Frank. Visies op een fenomeen*. Amsterdam/Antwerpen: De Prom, 2003.

Torrès, Tereska. *Les maisons hantées de Meyer Levin*. Paris: Éditions Denoël, 1991.

Waaldijk, Berteke. "Reading Anne Frank as a Woman." *Women's Studies International Forum*, vol. 16, no. 4, 327–335. Amsterdam: Elsevier, 1993.

Wallagh, Bob. *Verfilmd verleden. De camera's op het dagboek van Anne Frank*. Maastricht: Leiter-Nypels (z.j.).

Wesseling, Daphne. "Een onderzoek naar het beeld van Anne Frank in Japan tussen 1952 en heden." MA diss. Masterscriptie History of Society Erasmus Universiteit Rotterdam, 2010.

Wilson, Cara. *Love, Otto: The Legacy of Anne Frank*. Kansas City: Andrews McMeel Publishing, 1995.

Winters, Shelley. *Shelley 2: The Middle of My Century*. New York: Ballantine Books, 1989.

Young, James. *The Art of Memory: Holocaust Memorials in History*. New York: Prestel, 1994.

Zee, Nanda van der. *The Roommate of Anne Frank*. Soesterberg: Aspekt, 2003.

Zee, Sytze van der. *Vogelvrij. De jacht op de Joodse onderduiker*. Amsterdam: De Bezige Bij, 2010.

Index

DAVID BARNOUW is an independent scholar and emeritus researcher and former director of communications at the Dutch Institute for War, Holocaust, and Genocide Studies. He has been a visiting professor at UVM in Burlington twice. David is a prominent Anne Frank scholar with regular appearances on national and international media and writer of more than fifteen books and dozens of articles on World War II subjects.

JEANNETTE K. RINGOLD has translated over twenty fiction and nonfiction works by Dutch authors into English.

CPSIA information can be obtained
at www.ICGtesting.com
Printed in the USA
BVOW08s1129060318
509838BV00017B/616/P